CREATING BIOPHILIC BUILDINGS

An Ecotone Publishing Book 2017
Copyright ©2017 by the International Living Future Institute

ECOTONE PUBLISHING – AN IMPRINT OF INTERNATIONAL LIVING FUTURE INSTITUTE

All rights reserved. No part of this publication may be reproduced, distributed or transmit-ted in any form or by any means, including photocopying, recording, or other electronic or mechanical methods, without the prior written permission of the publisher, except in the case of brief quotations embodied in critical reviews and certain other noncommercial uses permitted by copyright law. For permission requests, write to the publisher, addressed "Attention Permissions Coordinator," at the address below.

For more information write:

Ecotone Publishing
1501 East Madison Street Suite 150,
Seattle 98122

AUTHOR: Amanda Sturgeon
BOOK DESIGN: softfirm
EDITED BY: Juliet Grable

LIBRARY OF CONGRESS CONTROL NUMBER: 2017949603

Library of Congress Cataloging-in Publication Data
ISBN: 978-0-9972368-3-5

1. ARCHITECTURE   2. PHILOSOPHY   3. ENVIRONMENT

First Edition

Printed in Canada on FSC-certified paper, processed Chlorine-Free, using vegetable-based ink.

TABLE OF CONTENTS:

Foreword
BY JUDITH HEERWAGEN   4

Acknowledgements   7

Introduction: Rediscovering Biophilic Design   8

CASE STUDIES:

Case Studies Through Time   18

Bertschi School Science Wing   32

Phipps Center for Sustainable Landscapes   42

Frick Environmental Center   52

Betty & Clint Josey Pavilion   64

R. W. Kern Center   74

Hawai'i Preparatory Academy Energy Lab   86

Mosaic Centre for Conscious Community and Commerce   96

VanDusen Botanical Garden Visitor Centre   108

David & Lucile Packard Foundation   120

Te Kura Whare   132

Glumac Shanghai Office   144

Sustainable Buildings Research Centre   154

Bullitt Center   166

Google Chicago   176

CONCLUSION:

Tools & Resources   190

About ILFI   204

Photo Credits   205

FOREWORD:
THE HUMAN-NATURE BOND IN THE BUILT ENVIRONMENT

BY JUDITH HEERWAGEN
AFFILIATE FACULTY, DEPARTMENT OF ARCHITECTURE, UNIVERSITY OF WASHINGTON

Creating Biophilic Buildings stands out. It is beautifully illustrated, but more importantly, it is a thoughtful and enlightening look at how teams make decisions about deep biophilic design. I use the term "deep" deliberately to call attention to the many connections that biophilic design should convey, but often does not. It is not a simple "how to" book. Each of the case studies deals with biophilic design differently, showing that there are many ways to reach the shared goal of reinforcing a connection and commitment to our inherited role as stewards of the natural world, even though we now live in a world largely of our own making.

The theme of connections is apparent, but expressed in different ways, for all of the case studies and intuitively shows how biophilic design is much like nature itself. Nature does not exist in a vacuum. Its components are related and connected in many ways — through time, space, and shared resources, as well as with other entities in natural ecosystems. And this book articulates how these natural connections have been central to the design and operation of the buildings it highlights. The connections are not just between the physical components of the space. They are also human connections linked to the special bonding that occurs between people when the project goals show what it means to be human and to care deeply about the environment and our place in it.

Nature as an organizing theme is apparent in all of the case studies. As Janine Benyus asks in her work on biomimicry: "How would nature do it?" While these case studies do not dwell on the functionality of natural systems, they do show how each of the projects and study teams look at the building as a system, taking cues from nature on where to direct our attention. The result is a view of buildings as a habitat of interconnected parts that together enable both people and surrounding landscapes to flourish.

Information richness runs through the case studies. Whether it is the use of daylight, links to the outdoors or interior design elements, there is a clear recognition that the environment can be a source of information that guides our behavior — whether it is through the light that changes with time and weather or the connection to seasonal change and variability.

Unlike many other books about design, this book conveys the thinking behind the biophilic design process, how design teams made decisions and what factors contributed most. This is highly valuable for all readers. It is not just a pretty picture book — although the photos and illustrations are indeed beautiful. It is a book that will inspire you to think about how the human-nature bond in the built environment can be nourished and sustained.

VanDusen Botanical Garden

ACKNOWLEDGEMENTS:

Creating this book was a collaborative effort and could not have happened without the support and passion of everyone involved. In particular, Juliet Grable, who was the co-writer and editor of this book, brought a thoughtful and eloquent voice to the challenging task of expressing multi-sensory experiences in words. Without the diligent and rigorous research skills of Edna Catumbela, this book would not have happened as she spent hours interviewing the teams and tracking down images and facts, always with grace and curiosity. It is thanks to the fine management skills of Michael Berrisford, Ecotone Publishing's Editor-in-Chief, that this book has come together rather than remaining an idea in my head. I also extend my gratitude to Erin Gehle and Johanna Björk for designing a beautiful book befitting the magical chemistry of nature and architecture combined.

The idea for this book came out of a retreat with the Biophilic Design Initiative group in December 2016 where it became apparent to me that our ability to advance biophilic design was pivoting around us being able to show building owners and designers what it meant to create a biophilic building. Thank you to Bill Browning, Judith Heerwagen, Vivian Loftness, Mary Davidge, Catie Ryan, David Gerson, Julia Africa and Nicole Isle for being allies in the Biophilic Design revolution; each of you inspires me greatly.

I am grateful to everyone involved with the projects featured in this book who were so generous with their time. They committed to interviews, shared images and became all-around cheerleaders for the project. I am honored to have such a great team and Board of Directors at ILFI. Every day it is a joy to work with them and witness the profound and positive change they make in the world. Lastly, but certainly not least, my children are my greatest inspiration for why I am driven to connect people to nature every day. Jarrah and Bee — you are my light.

AMANDA STURGEON, FAIA, 2017

Glumac Shanghai Office

INTRODUCTION: REDISCOVERING BIOPHILIC DESIGN

I had not given much thought to what an architect was before taking time off between high school and college to travel. As I backpacked through the Australian landscape, the sheer natural beauty of the country, its unique flora and fauna, and the vast expanses of pristine land stood in stark contrast to the developed cityscapes of England where I grew up. When I first set eyes on Sydney Harbor, for the first time in my life I could visualize a place where the natural world and built environment coexist and complement each other.

A few years later, as I traveled through Southeast Asia, I came to discover the unique history, ecology, and culture of each place through its buildings. It struck me that who we are as people has much to do with the intersection and mingling of nature and the human-built environment. This idea fascinated me. I wondered, what if the barriers between the two—between nature and people, between nature and buildings—could be dissolved? What if we felt the same experience walking through a city or a building as we did walking through a forest? This became my passion and my calling. I became an architect with the commitment to connect people and nature through the buildings I designed.

Biophilic design, or the deliberate incorporation of elements from nature into the built environment, is not a new practice. In every part of the world, and for millennia, people have infused architecture with plant and animal motifs, incorporated gardens, ponds, and atria into buildings and "brought the outside in" by keeping plants and animals close.

Examples of biophilic design abound, especially in indigenous architecture. The cedar houses built by Northwest Coast Indians in the Pacific Northwest are replete with compelling stylized images of orcas, ravens, eagles, beavers, and other creatures. The artwork reveals how deeply intertwined these creatures are with the people's cultural status, identity, and spirituality. Japanese timber-framed structures show a deep reverence for the trees and other materials used in their making. In the modern era, many of Frank Lloyd Wright's projects exhibit biophilic design, from Samara, which incorporates the winged seed motif in the home's clerestory windows and elsewhere, to Fallingwater, an exhilarating example of how a building can be integrated with its environment. On a larger scale, the revitalized Western Harbor neighborhood in Malmö, Sweden, incorporates meandering open water channels, waterfalls, gardens, and courtyards throughout. This green infrastructure not only treats stormwater; it infuses the city with beauty and the soothing presence of still and running water. This development also draws all of its energy from local and renewable sources.

There is a reason homes with "million-dollar views" go for a premium, and why most of us request the table next to the window at our favorite restaurant. Similarly, there is a reason we keep plants on our work desks and found natural objects such as shells on our nightstands and fall asleep to the soothing sound of ocean waves, even if that sound emanates from a white noise machine.

The foundations of human psychology rest on our instinctive reactions to the natural world. Our brains are evolutionarily preconditioned to seek out places that provide refuge while enabling us to look about and prospect—to consider what is coming next. We are predisposed to explore and discover nature, and we are physiologically wired to respond to the weather, the seasons and the time of day.

Most of us have experienced buildings that capture the movement of the sun through the sky. These dynamic shadows and pools of light that play across the floor connect us to the time of day, the season, and our sense of our inner biorhythm. There is a lasting and healing power in these moments, and they can serve as touchstones, whenever we need a respite from our busy and sometimes stressful lives.

But all too often, our contemporary buildings do not give us the chance to connect with nature. Buildings with few or no windows, no fresh air, and views of nothing, save a wall or a parking lot, are all too common. Given that we spend 90 percent of our time inside, this means many of us are living the majority of our lives completely cut off from the natural world—in a sense, cut off from a part of ourselves.

If, for as long as we have been building shelters, biophilic design has come naturally to us, how could this happen?

Like all living things, we are limited by our environment, but unlike other creatures, humans have developed technologies that allow us to push beyond our ecological and physiological constraints. Our clothing and shelters enable us to live in extreme climates; our global transportation network lets us enjoy a varied diet drawn from all parts of the world. Since the Industrial Revolution, our technologies have evolved ever more rapidly, and the constraints have all but fallen away. In most contemporary Western cultures, we use our buildings to assert domination over nature and highlight our separation from it. No longer must we rely on natural ventilation or orient our buildings to capture the sun's warmth or shade us from its swelter. Abundant and inexpensive energy has allowed us to create our own artificial and perfectly calibrated interior environments. Instead of actively managing these environments by manually opening windows or manipulating shades, we have become passive observers, reliant on systems that automatically control space heating and cooling. Much of the world is moving toward this Western model of overconsumption and constant comfort.

At the same time, a massive and global shift from agrarian to urban lifestyles is happening. Today, more than half of the world's population lives in urban environments, and the United Nations projects that by 2050 that number will grow to 66 percent. Although cities certainly have their strong points, it is all too easy to push nature aside in these human-built environments, and it becomes more difficult for people to see that they are directly dependent on the natural environment for the basic needs of food, clothing, shelter, water, and healthy air.

This growing disconnect has dire consequences. Like any relationship, our bond with the natural world requires nurturing. If we do not attend to it, this relationship can wither and die, leading to indifference or even contempt. We are already seeing the disastrous consequences of this estrangement in habitat destruction, species extinction, and pollution. Children who do not spend enough time outside are suffering from nature deficit disorder, which is associated with a host of physical, psychological and behavioral problems, including obesity, depression, and attention disorders.

Ironically, the implications of global climate change may, by necessity, urge us away from this destructive path and

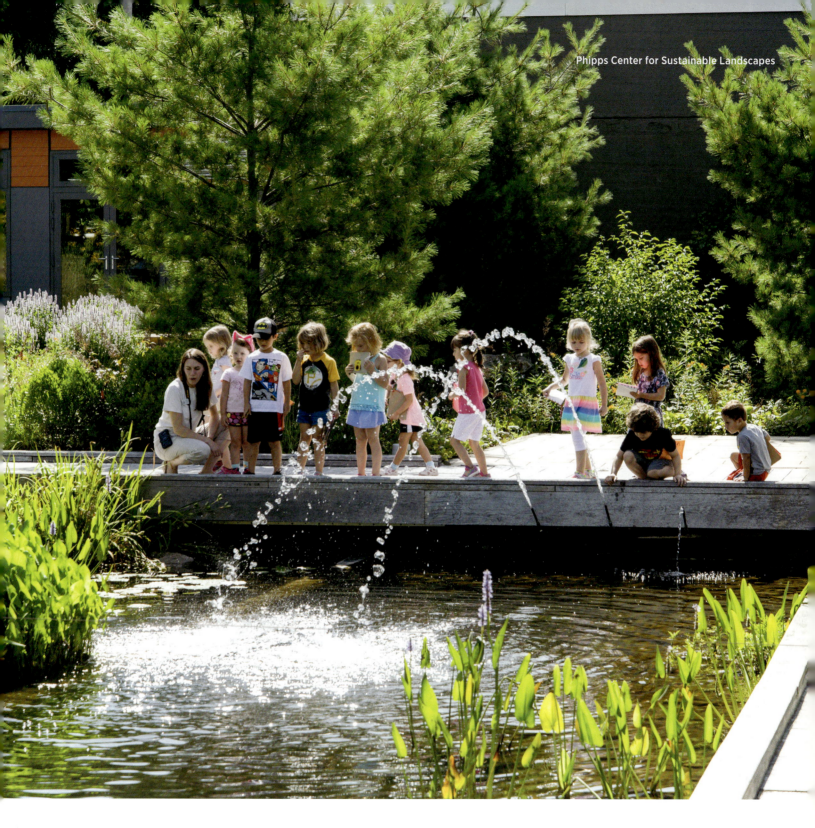

Bullitt Center

toward solutions which both consume fewer resources and help restore our connections with the natural world. We are making stepwise progress through more rigorous energy codes and the courageous leadership of many in the sustainable design community, but if we have any hope of meeting the goals established at the UN Climate Change Conference (COP21) in Paris in 2015, we will have to radically change our approach to designing buildings.

THE FOUNDINGS OF BIOPHILIC DESIGN

Biologist E.O. Wilson published *Biophilia* in 1984, in which he set forth the hypothesis that the human tendency to affiliate with other living things is encoded in our DNA, along with the hope that it would spur a renewed conservation ethic. Others built upon Wilson's ideas. Stephen Kellert, whose early work focused on the connections between nature and children's health and development, collaborated with Wilson on a series of publications and later pioneered the concept of biophilic design in architecture. Since Roger Ulrich published a study on hospital recovery rates being influenced by patients' contact with nature in 1984, several other studies have shown the link between access to nature and productivity, which can serve as a proxy for health and well-being. Pioneers in the philosophy and practice of biophilic design include

Vivian Loftness, who has coordinated research that quantifies the health and productivity benefits of biophilic design, and Judith Heerwagen, who co-edited *Biophilic Design* with Kellert. Heerwagen coined the term "bio-inspired design" to describe building interiors that draw from nature to the benefit of occupants.

In *Biophilic Design: The Theory, Science and Practice of Bringing Buildings to Life*, Stephen Kellert defines six elements and over seventy mechanisms for engendering a biophilic experience through building design. The Living Building Challenge Standard draws upon Kellert's work, and project teams must address each of these six biophilic elements to meet the Challenge's Biophilia Imperative. Others have developed slightly different frameworks; for example, Terrapin Bright Green outlines 14 Patterns of Biophilic Design in order to articulate the relationships among nature, science and the built environment. Bill Browning of Terrapin Bright Green has authored many articles and research reports that articulate the impacts of biophilic design.[1]

ACCELERATING THE SHIFT

Increasingly, green building project teams have attempted to incorporate biophilic design into their projects, but often their efforts amount to adding trees and plants or water features to their buildings. I believe this is because nothing in their training or backgrounds has prepared them for this exercise, and their experience with green building rating systems has trained them to fulfill the minimum requirements of a checklist without thinking past that step. True biophilic design goes much further and deeper, drawing on the intrinsic psychology that is mapped in our brains calling for us to be connected deeply to the natural world. Embedded within the Living Building Challenge program since the beginning, we are starting to see biophilic design explorations of a new rigor.

Although the frameworks developed by Kellert and others are helpful, there is no easy checklist to bring biophilic design into mainstream design practice; the principles do not translate easily into code language. This is because biophilic design is a philosophy that requires a shift in thinking. Though its benefits can be quantified, biophilic design draws as much from intuition and emotion as it does knowledge and formal training. It requires each individual to tap into the instinct that guides them to pay more for a home with a view of a park, the mountains or a lake, or to live on a street lined with trees.

How can we encourage this shift in thinking, one that inspires and instructs creators of buildings to think systematically, and to use biophilic design as the design driver instead of applying it as an afterthought? The long-view answer is that such a shift starts early, with children, at home and in schools, with parents and teachers who help foster the bonds between children and the natural world by encouraging exploration, play, and wonder. Simply spending time in natural landscapes and with plants and animals nurtures the relationship. And the good news is that, in some places, efforts to increase ecological literacy among the younger generation is rising. But what about aspiring architects and designers, and those who are already practicing?

First, those of us in the position to mentor young design professionals must change our approach. We must train architects and designers to think and act systematically and design holistically, and we must help them develop inspirational tools to communicate to building owners and developers the profound and positive impacts of biophilic design on building occupants. Some models and resources already exist. Organizations such as Terrapin Bright Green provide services intended to help restore the connections between people and the environment; for example, biophilic design workshops and charrettes lead design teams through creative thinking sessions, during which participants explore specific biophilic design strategies for improving health and wellness.

1 www.terrapinbrightgreen.com/publications

We at the International Living Future Institute believe that such a collaborative approach is key to propelling these ideas forward; consequently, we have invited leading experts in biophilic design to help launch the Biophilic Design Initiative, which aims to achieve broad adoption of Biophilic Design among the design community, building owners, and cities. Through this initiative, we are creating a repository for ideas, research, and collaborative opportunities. We will connect project teams with biophilic design practitioners and resources, and we will connect design practitioners with research scientists, all while compiling a research databank.

Equally important for accelerating this shift, we need built examples— projects that demonstrate how biophilic design, when used as the design driver, can positively transform both the design process and the resulting building environment for occupants. We need built examples that intentionally draw from our instinctual connection to nature. We need built examples that demonstrate the positive impacts of biophilic design on energy performance, comfort, health, and productivity.

Fortunately, with each passing year, we have more such projects. I was motivated to write this book to disseminate these examples to as many practitioners as possible, not only to showcase the results but to illuminate the process. The following case studies vary in scope, climate zone, setting, and other particularities. Each draws on the specificity of place—its climate, ecology, culture, and landscape—to create rich, nurturing built environments that support occupants' health and feed their yearning for connection. These buildings are a starting point on the pathway to creating truly biophilic buildings, and they provide us with clear examples, methodologies, and lessons learned.

For each case study, I use Stephen Kellert's framework of Biophilic Design Elements and Attributes to elucidate the project's biophilic design achievements. I believe that Kellert's list, created in collaboration with Judith Heerwagen and others, is the most thorough framework we have, and working with it can help building professionals embrace a new design philosophy. As we approach our drawing boards, this framework provides a place to start thinking about how to create places where people and nature can thrive together. This is a new way of thinking for most architects, designers and owners and developers of buildings, but embracing this approach is completely mandatory if the human species is to survive, and what is more thrive, on this planet.

Te Kura Whare

"I roamed Frick Park for many years... The deepest ravine, over which loomed the Forbes Avenue bridge, was called Fern Hollow. There in winter I searched for panther tracks in the snow. In summer and fall I imagined the woods extending infinitely. I was the first human being to see these shadowed trees, this land; I would make my pioneer clearing here, near the water... In spring I pried flat rocks from the damp streambed and captured red and black salamanders." ANNIE DILLARD, AN AMERICAN CHILDHOOD, 1987

CASE STUDIES THROUGH TIME

Humans have been practicing biophilic design for thousands of years. Through the millennia, people have built shelters with the resources they had available and in response to their particular climate. These shelters served practical functions: they helped people stay warm or cool, protected them from sun, rain, and weather, and helped them preserve food and other possessions. But these dwellings often did much more. They were expressions of culture, reinforcing and reflecting people's traditions and spiritual beliefs. They responded to the place in a unique way.

Not all of this knowledge has been lost in the practice of modern architecture. Architects such as Frank Lloyd Wright dedicated their careers to creating climate-adaptive and place-based buildings such as the iconic residence Fallingwater. Integrated into a waterfall in a lush forested setting in rural Pennsylvania, Fallingwater is a beautiful example of a building that was created in response to its unique site and which promotes interactions between people and nature.

In the process of designing the Sydney Opera House, architect Jørn Utzon studied the interactions between people and the water's edge before ever putting pen to paper. His winning

Fallingwater

Gurunsi Earth Houses of Burkina Faso

Sydney Opera House

design, which features dramatic white "sails" that evoke the boats on the water and the movement of waves and clouds, created an iconic building that Australians proudly embrace as a cultural symbol. Not only does the Sydney Opera House incorporate natural forms, it fosters a gradual and deepening relationship between people and nature. As visitors approach, they engage on a path of continual ascension, up the exterior steps and into the underside of the soaring sails. As they continue up a series of steps on the way to the performance halls, openings between the sails provide tantalizing glimpses of the harbor. The journey from street to musical experience continually reinforces the relationship to place.

Indigenous architecture holds many lessons about how to create shelters that are formed in response to climate by using the resources that nature provides. These structures, built from locally sourced materials and in response to the sun, wind, and water conditions of the particular place, exemplify biophilic design.

GURUNSI EARTH HOUSES

The Gurunsi are one of many ethnic groups in the region that includes southern Burkina Faso and northern Ghana in western Africa. Their earth houses are excellent examples of structures that utilize readily available materials while also providing an

CASE STUDIES THROUGH TIME | 21

Cliff dwellings at Mesa Verde

avenue for cultural expression. These round and rectilinear dwellings are made from a mixture of clay, straw, and cow droppings, which the men mix by foot.

The Gurunsi people have adapted their homes to the harsh climate, constructing thick walls with few openings, which keeps them cool during the hot day and comfortable during the cool night. What makes these dwellings unique are the elaborate paintings that adorn every square inch of the exterior. Using paint made from a mixture of water, mud, cow dung, and colored soil or chalk, the Gurunsi decorate their dwellings with symbolic patterns, scenes from daily life, and animal motifs. Each home features a unique and meaningful design.

MESA VERDE CLIFF DWELLINGS

Located in southwest Colorado, the cliff dwellings at Mesa Verde provide a window into the Pueblo Indian people, their way of life, and their amazing architectural minds.

Constructed almost nine hundred years ago, these dwellings were built into high alcoves along the canyon walls and are astonishingly well preserved. The structures, which number over six hundred, range from small storage rooms to elaborate complexes with between fifty and two hundred rooms.

Native American Teepee

Cliff dwellings at Mesa Verde

Built with adobe, and later, with stone, mud, and wood beams, these ancient feats of engineering and construction persevered in a climate that includes heavy snows, thunderstorms, and extreme dry heat. Cliff Palace, the largest dwelling at Mesa Verde, demonstrated passive solar design centuries before modern-day practitioners embraced the approach. A massive rock overhang keeps the entire set of dwellings cool and shades them from the hot desert sun, while the thermal mass of the walls helps to moderate interior temperatures.

NATIVE AMERICAN HOUSES
American Indians built many types of dwellings throughout North America, each reflecting a specific tribe's lifestyle and regional climate. From wigwams and tepees to longhouses and grass houses, these structures varied in materiality and form, but they were all made with earth-based materials and fashioned with an attitude of respect for the land.

The Algonquian Indians, who ranged throughout the woodlands of New England and Eastern Canada, built wigwams. These small, easy-to-construct domed dwellings consist of a wooden frame covered with woven mats and sheets of birch bark. Ropes were used to wrap the mats and hold the birch bark in place.

The Iroquois built longhouses. Although structurally similar to wigwams, longhouses could measure up to two hundred feet long and house as many as sixty people—a cultural expression of the Iroquois' community values. In contrast to these permanent structures, the nomadic Plains tribes constructed tepees. These highly portable shelters consist of a cone-like frame made with long wooden poles that was then covered in hide, typically buffalo. Adept at shedding both wind and rain, tepees were convenient and comfortable houses for people who moved frequently as they followed the buffalo herds.

These few examples of Native American houses show how indigenous people retained the connection to the land while meeting their physical and cultural needs. Designs shaped by climate, available building materials, and the lifestyles of the people themselves, these shelters illustrate the ingenious ways humans adapt to unique circumstances, rather than imposing designs on the landscape regardless of environmental conditions or constraints.

While these examples have inspired architects around the world, the lessons contained within them do not impact the average building built today. Most conventional buildings constructed in the industrialized parts of the world are designed with cost as the main driver; however, while budget is a constraint on every project, good design considers a myriad of factors that work in concert: energy performance, aesthetics, material choices, relationships to the site and neighborhood, and programming needs. Biophilic design goes a step further and considers how all of these design decisions can promote the health and well-being of the building's occupants by connecting them with nature.

As the fourteen case studies presented here illustrate, biophilic design is ultimately about making happier, healthier spaces where both people and nature can thrive.

Native American Longhouse

Betty & Clint Josey Pavilion

INTRODUCTION TO THE CASE STUDIES

Upon investigating resources related to biophilic design, I discovered that only four case studies were currently available to the general public. Architects and designers, who are almost all overwhelmingly visual learners, must be able to draw inspiration from precedents. If we want practitioners to embrace biophilic design as both a design philosophy and as a process, we need case studies that illustrate how to achieve it practically and elegantly.

This contemporary collection of fourteen case studies draws from Living Building Challenge projects.

Since 2011, the Living Building Challenge has required that all projects utilize Stephen Kellert's framework to achieve biophilic design—the only green building standard that includes biophilic design as a requirement. Consequently, the projects that are now built and operating as Living Buildings provide a significant resource for the advancement of biophilic design.

Additionally, Version 3.1 of the Living Building Challenge requires that projects hold a one-day biophilic design exploration and create a guiding framework for the project based on the criteria outlined on the following page. This requirement influenced some of the fourteen case studies as well.

Some of the projects were also influenced by other approaches to biophilic design, such as Terrapin Bright Green's *14 Patterns of Biophilic Design*, which coalesces Kellert's attributes into fourteen patterns organized within three groups. Although this framework and Terrapin's extensive resources are pivotal tools for advancing the practice of biophilic design, for the sake of consistency we have not specifically referenced them within these case studies.

The case studies do not focus on the other Living Building Challenge Imperatives; however, it is worth mentioning that most of these projects have achieved some to all of the requirements set forth in the Living Building Challenge standard: they are net zero or net positive for energy and/or water use; they are constructed with materials free of Red List items; they demonstrate the principles of equity; they are respectful of place; and they are beautiful.

Because the Living Building Challenge requires projects to reference and respond to the Biophilic Design Elements and Attributes list that Stephen R. Kellert published in the 2008 book *Biophilic Design*[2]*: The Theory and Practice of Bringing Buildings to Life*, I have organized the case studies according to that list (see the full list on pages 28-29).

In analyzing this group of projects against Kellert's elements and attributes, I have come to appreciate even more how comprehensive and thoughtful this list is. The attributes cover the range of biophilic expression, from the basic human need for natural light and fresh air to our more complex emotional yearning to connect with our cultures, our histories, and the natural environment.

[2] Stephen R. Kellert, Judith H. Heerwagen, and Martin L. Mador, *Biophilic Design: The Theory, Science, and Practice of Bringing Buildings to Life* (Hoboken: John Wiley & Sons, 2008), Table 1.1, p15

LIVING BUILDING CHALLENGE
IMPERATIVE 09: BIOPHILIC ENVIRONMENT

The project must be designed to include elements that nurture the innate human/nature connection. Each project team must engage in a minimum of one all-day exploration of the biophilic design potential for the project. The exploration must result in a biophilic framework and plan for the project that outlines the following:

- How the project will be transformed by deliberately incorporating nature through Environmental Features, Light and Space, and Natural Shapes and Forms

- How the project will be transformed by deliberately incorporating nature's patterns through Natural Patterns and Processes and Evolved Human-Nature Relationships

- How the project will be uniquely connected to the place, climate, and culture through Place-Based Relationships

- The provision of sufficient and frequent human-nature interactions in both the interior and exterior of the project to connect the majority of occupants with nature directly

The plan must contain methods for tracking biophilia at each design phase. The plan should include historical, cultural, ecological, and climatic studies that thoroughly examine the site and context for the project.

living-future.org/lbc

KELLERT'S BIOPHILIC DESIGN ELEMENTS & ATTRIBUTES

ENVIRONMENTAL FEATURES

Color
Water
Air
Natural ventilation
Plants
Animals
Natural materials
Views and vistas
Façade greening
Geology and landscape
Habitats and ecosystems
Fire

NATURAL SHAPES + FORMS

Botanical motifs
Tree and columnar supports
Animal (mainly vertebrate) motifs
Shells and spirals
Egg, oval and tubular forms
Arches, vaults, domes
Shapes resisting straight lines and right angles
Simulation of natural features
Biomorphy
Geomorphology
Biomimicry

NATURAL PATTERNS + PROCESSES

Sensory variability
Information richness
Age, change and the patina of time
Growth and efflorescence
Central focal point
Patterned wholes
Bounded spaces
Transitional spaces
Linked series and chains
Integration of parts to wholes
Complementary contrasts
Dynamic balance and tension
Fractals
Hierarchically organized ratios and scales

The element of Light and Space includes a full exploration of the ways in which light and space interact to promote biophilic experiences. The element of Natural Shapes and Forms reveals why we find arches, domes, spirals, curves, and other naturalistic features so intriguing, and why these features so often find their way into our buildings. If you have not already,

I encourage you to become intimately familiar with these elements and attributes and have no doubt you will come to appreciate them as I have.

Each case study illustrates two or three elements from Kellert's list and describes in detail how the project addresses three attributes listed under those selected elements.

I selected attributes based on extensive interviews with the design teams, owners, and occupants, as well as from their own narratives and presentations describing their approach to biophilic design. In most cases, I also conducted an in-person site visit. The attributes discussed during the interviews were not always the ones I selected. For example, with one project it was clear to me that

LIGHT + SPACE

Natural light
Filtered and diffused light
Light and shadow
Reflected light
Light pools
Warm light
Light as shape and form
Spaciousness
Spatial variability
Space as shape and form
Spatial harmony
Inside-outside spaces

PLACE-BASED RELATIONSHIPS

Geographic connection to place
Historic connection to place
Ecological connection to place
Cultural connection to place
Indigenous materials
Landscape orientation
Landscape features that define building form
Landscape ecology
Integration of culture and ecology
Spirit of place
Avoiding placelessness

EVOLVED HUMAN-NATURE RELATIONSHIPS

Prospect and refuge
Order and complexity
Curiosity and enticement
Change and metamorphosis
Security and protection
Mastery and control
Affection and attachment
Attraction and beauty
Exploration and discovery
Information and cognition
Fear and awe
Reverence and spirituality

---

connection to place and climate drove the design, yet strangely, the design team did not mention these influences.

Several projects embraced biophilic design more fully and illustrated more than the three elements we chose to feature. However, in order to show a range of examples and strategies, I selected the elements and attributes that both tell a good story about biophilic design and provide valuable lessons learned.

Viewing these case studies as a group has been illuminating. Some projects have been more successful than others at integrating biophilic design into their design generation and conceptual development, and the inclusion of a specific case study does not imply that it is exemplary in every category of biophilic design. It is important to acknowledge that these design teams are also on a journey to understand and discover how biophilic design can inform their practices. The key takeaway is to recognize the potential that biophilic design can bring to our buildings, both now and in the future.

"If facts are the seeds that later produce knowledge and wisdom, then the emotions and impressions of the senses are the fertile soil in which the seeds must grow. The early years of childhood are the time to prepare the soil." RACHEL CARSON

BERTSCHI SCHOOL

PART I:
ENGAGING THE SENSES

PROJECT NAME:
BERTSCHI SCHOOL SCIENCE WING

BUILDING TYPE:
EDUCATIONAL

LOCATION:
SEATTLE, WASHINGTON

BUILDING SQUARE FOOTAGE:
5,225 SQ. FT.

OWNER:
THE BERTSCHI SCHOOL

ARCHITECT:
KMD ARCHITECTS

LANDSCAPE ARCHITECT:
GGLO

ENGINEER:
RUSHING

SUSTAINABILITY CONSULTANT:
O'BRIEN & COMPANY

CONTRACTOR:
SKANSKA USA BUILDING, INC.

SPECIAL THANK YOU TO:

STAN RICHARDSON, OWNER'S REPRESENTATIVE, BERTSCHI SCHOOL

MARK SINDALL, LANDSCAPE ARCHITECT, GGLO

STACY SMEDLEY, DESIGNER, CO-PROJECT MANAGER

Bertschi School students contributed their ideas about bringing nature into their new science building.

PART II: DESIGN PROCESS

The Bertschi School Science Wing serves as a hands-on earth science classroom for kindergarten through fifth-grade students. Consisting of a classroom, attached greenhouse and outdoor garden space, it was designed for—and in part by—elementary school children. The project demonstrates how biophilic design can be used to not only connect children with natural processes, but engage them in learning.

The team involved the students in the design process early on by asking them how they wanted to see nature expressed in their new classroom. Unconstrained by the realities of budgets and architectural conventions, the children gave their imaginations free rein. Their simple requests reflect the innate yearning for the natural world: a river running through the classroom; views of the sky; a greenhouse full of plants growing all year round.

Many of the children's ideas became central elements in the final design. The "indoor river" forms an integral part of the rainwater collection system. A wall of plants lines the tallest wall of the EcoHouse, a greenhouse space that also houses the water treatment equipment. And an ethnobotanical garden just outside the classroom allows the students to care for, harvest, and use native plants, connecting them not only with the natural world here and now, but with the Duwamish people who originally inhabited the region.

> "The school already had the commitment to teaching nature. We decided we had to find a way for every system or component that's helping us show how a building uses sun, or water, or the environment around it to be a learning opportunity for students, because it's an educational space."
>
> **STACY SMEDLEY**

PART III: BUILT EXPERIENCE

The Bertschi School Science Wing demonstrates how successful biophilic design engages all of the senses. In this hands-on educational setting, children are encouraged to touch the plants. They can hear the gentle trickle of water coursing gently through the runnel; they notice the change in humidity as they enter the EcoHouse, where plants on the wall breathe out life-giving oxygen and transpire water. They can see textures of the plants on the living wall, and they can press their hands into the imprints of salmon "swimming" across the floor alongside the runnel and run their fingers across the leaves imprinted in the concrete.

The children experience these features both consciously and unconsciously. Because so many of the biophilic elements were designed with integrated functions and hands-on learning in mind, students interact with many of them in their daily lessons.

"The metaphor of the flower was a great starting point because it meant that we weren't just thinking about how we're going to plug in certain aspects of nature, but how the whole building is acting like a natural thing."
STACY SMEDLEY

"We set out to really demonstrate the living processes of nature and then express those through every aspect of the project. We worked hard to distill these down into simple understandable things that you could touch and feel."
MARK SINDALL

"Essential to this project's success was using nature and visualizing nature as an organizing framework for design, not just for the designer but for anyone that is going to be experiencing the space. The challenge is shifting to that alternative way of thinking. Once you've shifted, it actually makes the process way more fun and the outcome is something more people appreciate."
STACY SMEDLEY

PART IV: BIOPHILIC ELEMENTS + ATTRIBUTES

ENVIRONMENTAL FEATURES

WATER: Seattle is a place of rain and water. The Bertschi School is located on a steep hill where the rain rushes down the urban streets to reach Lake Union. Children who grow up in the Pacific Northwest are used to splashing through puddles on their way to school and arriving with wet feet and faces. In this region, buildings provide both refuge from the rain and protected spaces from which to watch and enjoy it. Given this reality, it is not surprising that the kids at Bertschi asked for a river running through the building.

When the rain starts to run down the "stream," the kids immediately run to observe; they reach out to touch the glass and follow the flow

of water as it makes it way to the cistern and raingarden. More than just a water feature, the stream celebrates a connection to place and encourages exploration and discovery.

AIR: Buildings in the mild climate of Seattle can be naturally ventilated during all seasons except for winter. Because it was an addition to an existing building, the science classroom's access to sunlight was limited, but the design makes the most of the tight urban site with creative forms that effectively capture daylight.

In the classroom, the butterfly roof promotes a natural stack effect and provides natural ventilation and daylight for the space through a row of high windows. The greenhouse unabashedly celebrates the power of glass and sun to create a semi-tropical ecosystem that is in striking contrast to those typical of the cool Pacific Northwest. Even on an overcast day, students can enter the EcoHouse and feel the combination of captured solar energy and humidity from the transpiring plants on their faces and arms.

PLANTS: The living wall in the EcoHouse grew directly out of the students' request for "plants growing everywhere." Though living walls are sometimes installed simply as pleasant features, the plants on this wall serve a greater purpose: they treat and thrive on greywater from the building as they clean and oxygenate the air, engaging and instructing students on the water cycle and the ecological role plants play in capturing nutrients. Two moss-mat green roofs also provide a natural cover to approximately half of the building; these can be viewed by students in the adjacent classroom, which is oriented above the science classroom's roof line.

"The river is a beautiful idea; it's kind of poetic, and it's coming from these eight-year-olds. You have these beautiful ways of trying to get forms and functions that are natural into things that are typically square and flat, and the biggest one was putting a curvy thing full of water in the floor of our building on purpose. That's typically not a design strategy that we would think of ourselves."

STACY SMEDLEY

"If you take the beauty and the interaction out of it, you take the emotional connection out of it, and if you take the emotional connection out of it, you take the ingrained value of stewardship out of the minds of the kids. I think it would be a much less powerful building without these interactive features."

MARK SINDALL

Besides cleaning the air and filtering greywater, the green wall is a learning tool for students.

EVOLVED HUMAN-NATURE RELATIONSHIPS

EXPLORATION + DISCOVERY:

The design was grounded in the notion that nature is intellectually as well as physically and spiritually stimulating. The varied textures, shapes, and colors stimulate the children's innate curiosity, and every day Bertschi School students learn how features that are elegant and beautiful in form also function beautifully as well. The plants on the living wall filter greywater from the classroom's sinks and naturally purify the air. The runnel transports rainwater collected from the building's metal roof to the cistern, engaging students in the hydrological cycle. The plants in the ethnobotanical garden, so pleasing to look at, also provide food and useful materials for making things.

CHANGE + METAMORPHOSIS:

The building integrates natural systems and processes; consequently, change and metamorphosis are not only implied, but experienced directly. The students engage with the changing flows of water within the runnel and interact with the plants as they grow, flower, fruit, and sometimes die. Students harvest the edible plants and they engage with the seasons as the roof mosses change color and bloom, and as wind-blown seeds sprout and take root alongside them. They notice as the electrical demand of their classroom changes and as passing clouds affect the electricity generated by the solar array. No matter where the students look, the natural elements of the Bertschi Science building are always changing—just like the students themselves.

PHIPPS CENTER FOR SUSTAINABLE LANDSCAPES

42 | CREATING BIOPHILIC BUILDINGS

PART I: RISING FROM THE LANDSCAPE

PROJECT NAME:
PHIPPS CENTER FOR SUSTAINABLE LANDSCAPES

BUILDING TYPE:
EDUCATIONAL/ COMMERCIAL

LOCATION:
PITTSBURGH, PENNSYLVANIA

BUILDING SQUARE FOOTAGE:
24,350 SQ. FT.

OWNER:
PHIPPS CONSERVATORY AND BOTANICAL GARDENS

ARCHITECT:
THE DESIGN ALLIANCE ARCHITECTS

LANDSCAPE ARCHITECT:
ANDROPOGON

SUSTAINABILITY CONSULTANT:
EVOLVEEA, 7GROUP

SPECIAL THANK YOU TO:

SONJA BOCHART, BETA PROJECT MANAGER

RICHARD PIACENTINI, EXECUTIVE DIRECTOR, PHIPPS CONSERVATORY AND BOTANICAL GARDENS

The gardens surrounding the Center emulate natural landscapes, including wetlands.

PART II: DESIGN PROCESS

Part of the greater Phipps Conservatory and Botanical Gardens in Pittsburgh, Pennsylvania, the Center for Sustainable Landscapes was built to further the Conservatory's mission: to advance sustainability and promote human and environmental well-being through action and research. The Center serves as an educational and research facility and welcomes close to 450,000 visitors each year.

The steeply sloped brownfield site posed a major design challenge. Through an integrated design process that included bimonthly day-long charrettes, the project team, which included the project owners, focused on creating a structure that enhances its surroundings and always maintains a connection to the outdoors. This was accomplished by nestling the three-story building into the slope and orienting its east-west axis toward the southwest. A major goal was to carry over the experiential theme of the Conservatory and to connect the upper campus to this new site below. The team achieved this connection by designing terraced gardens and a winding footpath that leads from the roof down to the ground floor, inviting visitors to enter and exit the building at all three levels.

PART III: BUILT EXPERIENCE

The Center for Sustainable Landscapes serves as a respite for urban dwellers. Visitors approach the building from the upper campus above the site, meandering through terraced gardens that seem to embrace the building.

Inside, an open, light-filled atrium facilitates airflow and helps visitors stay attuned to the outside, as sounds reflecting the weather, season, and time of day filter through the space. The art installations help create a richly layered experience, connecting visitors with the region's ecology and history. Staff and visitors alike are invited to thread a length of yarn through the Skywatcher Loom and gaze up toward the sky, taking a moment to enjoy the tactile experience and build upon the work of others. In the light-filled lobby, access to the sky lifts the spirit, even on a dreary winter's day, and in the open offices, employees enjoy the many plants, abundant natural light, and fresh air.

> "I think it's really important to engage a biophilic design consultant who can work with your team. Think about what biophilic design elements make the most sense for this place, this purpose, and this time."
>
> **RICHARD PIACENTINI**

> "We were looking to reach people in different manners, to provide a diverse experience for the staff and visitors. Different people connect to different artworks with their own unique backgrounds and experiences. Diversity was key: having a multitude of materials; having different 'languages' that tell different stories."
>
> **SONJA BOCHART**

PART IV: BIOPHILIC ELEMENTS + ATTRIBUTES

ENVIRONMENTAL FEATURES

PLANTS: Incorporating over 150 native plants grouped into natural communities, the terraced gardens surround the building, even extending onto it with a green roof. The design creates outdoor rooms that blur the edges between building and landscape. The experience carries over inside the building, where the many windows provide intimate views of the gardens and live plants grace the offices, conference room, and lobby.

GEOLOGY + LANDSCAPE: The backdrop for this project is a dramatically sloping hillside. The Center, set into this bluff, becomes part of the geology. The gardens surrounding the building unfold in a series of planted areas that mimic the region's varied landscapes. As visitors approach the building from the upper campus and meander down the path toward the ground floor, the plantings, building, and topography work together to create natural-seeming transitions between outside and inside. Visitors pass by upland species at the roof level and through oak woodlands on the path, finally reaching wetlands and raingardens at the bottom of the slope.

VIEWS + VISTAS: To be in the Center is to be simultaneously outside. Every place in the building, including the classroom, conference room, offices, and three levels of the lobby provides distinctive perspectives and views: to the south and west, the expansive vista overlooking Panther Hollow and Junction Hollow; to the east, intimate views of the gardens; and to the north, views of the dramatic topography from which the building itself emerges.

Visitors can enter and exit the building on all three levels.

CASE STUDY: PHIPPS CENTER FOR SUSTAINABLE LANDSCAPES | 47

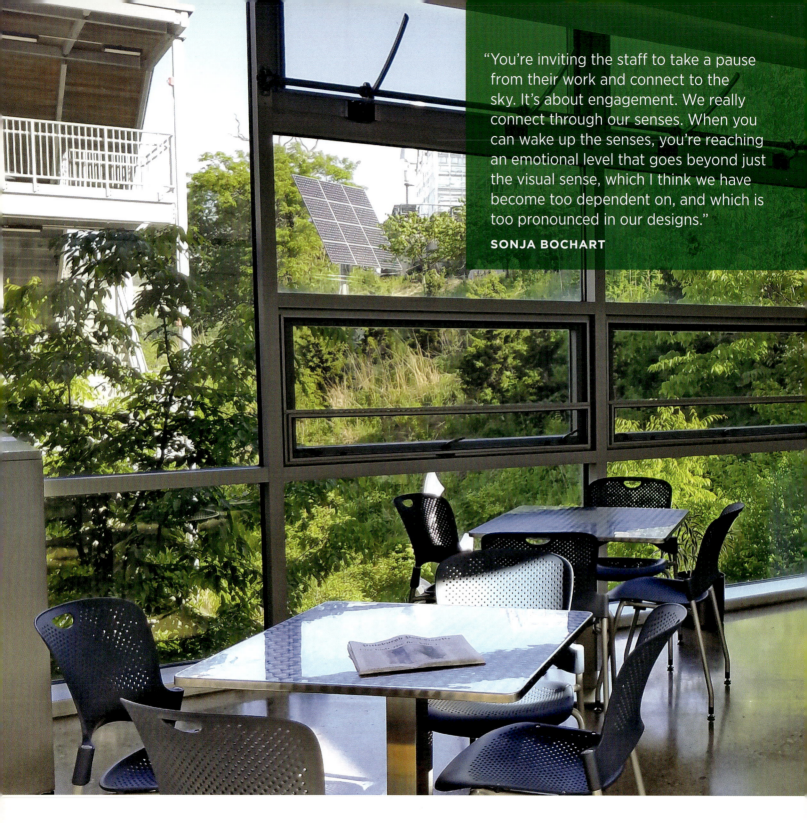

"You're inviting the staff to take a pause from their work and connect to the sky. It's about engagement. We really connect through our senses. When you can wake up the senses, you're reaching an emotional level that goes beyond just the visual sense, which I think we have become too dependent on, and which is too pronounced in our designs."

SONJA BOCHART

Large operable windows bring the scents and sounds of the gardens into the building.

NATURAL PATTERNS + PROCESSES

SENSORY VARIABILITY: This building takes advantage of its immersion in a botanical landscape, building on the dynamic variety of colors, textures, and shapes of the plants to bring an ever-changing visual and auditory experience to occupants. Recognizing the importance of sound to connect people to nature, Abby Arresty's audial sculpture brings the sounds of Pittsburgh—from the rhythmic whir of cicadas to the gentle patter of rain to the nostalgic whistle of a passing train—into the space, while interactive and three-dimensional art throughout the building stimulates eyes and minds. All of this sensory variability invites people to pause, touch, look, and listen—to connect with nature, but also with themselves.

CENTRAL FOCAL POINT: The Center is organized around a central lobby with an atrium, a feature that highlights the dramatic elevation change that characterizes the site. The three-story atrium anchors the building, serving as a guidepost for people whether they are inside or outside. Visitors who take the meandering path through the gardens can refer to this prominent feature—the translucent tower with its distinctive pitched roof is the highest point on the building—to stay oriented as they transition from the amphitheater down to the lagoon. Inside, the lobby and atrium orient people within the building and connect them to other spaces; from here, it is possible to see clear through the building from east to west. People are drawn to this light-filled public space, where sunlight, access to views, and art reinforce the atrium's function as the central focal point.

Natural light, art installations, and the sounds of nature combine to create a rich sensory experience inside the building.

INFORMATION RICHNESS: Inside the building, light, art, and sound combine to create a multilayered experience. Art installations inspired by nature enrich the interior and invite staff and visitors alike to pause. Glass sculptures that evoke colorful flowers bloom along one wall. A bronze windbell at the entry to the rooftop garden captures the movement of air in its clear, resonant tones. A suspended steel sculpture of curving steel bands draws attention with its contrasts of light and dark, solidity and air. The interplay of light drawn through the light shelves and atrium windows lifts the spirit. And the sound sculpture, filling the lobby with the sounds of insects, frogs, rain, and birdsong, echoes the season, weather, and time of day. Such richness not only stimulates the senses, but connects people with their emotions and memories.

CASE STUDY: PHIPPS CENTER FOR SUSTAINABLE LANDSCAPES | 51

FRICK ENVIRONMENTAL CENTER

PART I: ESTABLISHING A CONNECTION BETWEEN PEOPLE AND NATURE

PROJECT NAME:
FRICK ENVIRONMENTAL CENTER

BUILDING TYPE:
COMMERCIAL/ EDUCATIONAL

LOCATION:
PITTSBURGH, PENNSYLVANIA

BUILDING SQUARE FOOTAGE:
15,500 SQ. FT.

OWNER:
THE CITY OF PITTSBURGH & PITTSBURGH PARKS CONSERVANCY

ARCHITECT:
BOHLIN CYWINSKI JACKSON

LANDSCAPE ARCHITECT:
LAQUATRA BONCI ASSOCIATES

CONSTRUCTION MANAGEMENT:
P.J. DICK

SUSTAINABILITY CONSULTANT:
EVOLVEEA & ATELIER TEN

SPECIAL THANK YOU TO:

PATRICIA CULLEY, PROJECT ARCHITECT, BCJ

ROBERT AUMER, PROJECT MANAGER, BCJ

STEVE CHAITOW, PRINCIPAL, BCJ

LARRY JONES, ENVIRONMENTAL DESIGNER, ATELIER TEN

> "When we create a sense of wonder in architecture we become more open to ideas and experiences. The architecture serves the purpose of the Conservancy — to get people to be open to the message the Conservancy has to give."
>
> **STEVE CHAITOW**

PART II: DESIGN PROCESS

The Frick Environmental Center serves as a setting for hands-on environmental education and as the gateway to Frick Park, which at 644 acres, is Pittsburgh's largest park. The Center was built to replace a building that had been vandalized by arson and defaced with graffiti. The Pittsburgh Parks Conservancy approached the project with the intention of turning a cycle of deterioration into a cycle of stewardship, and the new building was to invite visitors to develop a deeper connection with the park and its cultural and natural history.

With project goals so closely aligned with biophilic design, the team deliberately incorporated biophilic features into the building early on. Instead of attempting to incorporate several elements at once, the team sought to create focused experiences through specific design features, creating a sequence of experiences that connect people with different aspects of nature and with the landscape and ecology of Frick Park.

Building orientation played a key role. The Center is perched on the edge of a south-facing slope. A carefully choreographed entry sequence helps visitors transition from the urban to the forest environment, and the windows and decks on the southern façade immerse occupants in the tree canopy. Interactive features that combine form, function, and art, such as the Rain Veil and Rain Ravine, engage visitors and spark curiosity.

The entry sequence was designed to lift visitors into the building before exposing them to the forest canopy.

PART III: BUILT EXPERIENCE

The new center establishes a place for people and nature to connect through the building, in the midst of the largest and wildest of Pittsburgh's parks. Visitors approach the Frick Environmental Center through historic gateways that were restored as part of the larger building project. From the sidewalk, they ascend up a narrow stepped path to the entry. Here views are momentarily compressed, but once inside the classrooms and public living room, tall vertical windows connect visitors with inspiring views of the forest canopy. When it rains, children run outside to watch rain cascade from the roof and down across the sandstone ledges of the Rain Ravine. Through these features, the Frick Center provides a multi-sensory experience that orients people in the landscape and prepares them to explore the streams, forests, ravines, and hills of Frick Park. The hope is that the children who fall in love with this special place will grow into adults who will treasure it and reinvest in its preservation.

The Rain Ravine demonstrates the erosive power of water.

> "Biophilia is about re-establishing the connection between nature and humans within the built environment; it's very much tied to the built environment, and it can happen in either abstract or literal ways."
> **PATRICIA CULLEY**

> "One thing we're seeing that is very helpful is to conduct a session with the client and the consultant that is just devoted to biophilia. In those sessions we've been doing two things: educating everyone on what biophilia and biophilic design mean; and second, having a 'blue-sky' session where everyone participates. You'd be amazed at what comes out."
> **STEVE CHAITOW**

> "Biophilia changed the team dynamic in that it gave us a common topic to rally around. Because we're all human beings."
> **STEVE CHAITOW**

PART IV: BIOPHILIC ELEMENTS + ATTRIBUTES

The Rain Veil captures the dramatic beauty of a rainstorm.

PLACE-BASED RELATIONSHIPS

LANDSCAPE ECOLOGY: The Center treats all of its own stormwater and wastewater on site and reinforces natural patterns of water flow. The roof collects stormwater but does not direct it into downspouts; instead, rain cascades from the roof in a dramatic forty-foot "veil." From there, rainwater collects and flows across the Rain Ravine, a series of sculpted sandstone ledges designed by artist Stacy Levy. This installation expresses the erosive power of water and reminds visitors of the connections between falling rain, the flow of water through the landscape, and healthy creeks and rivers. After passing through the Rain Ravine, water flows into a raingarden and ultimately, into Nine-Mile Creek.

The Frick Center serves as a gateway to the greater ecology of Frick Park.

INTEGRATION OF CULTURE + ECOLOGY: The Frick Center fits into the ecology and aesthetics of Frick Park. The integral structure does not take away from the environment, but instead fosters an openness and curiosity about the natural surroundings. The up-canted roof, designed to emulate a delicate falling leaf, encourages people to look outward with open minds and hearts. The long, tall windows and vertical wood siding mimic the pattern of tree trunks in a forest. Entering and exiting the building is a transformative experience. Visitors transition from an ordinary sidewalk and ascend a narrow path to the entry bridge. Once inside the building, visitors experience the tree canopy and engage with learning opportunities that teach them about the ecology and natural features of the park. As people exit the building, they cross a bridge and enter the greater Frick Park, ready to experience the forest in a more attentive way.

CASE STUDY: FRICK ENVIRONMENTAL CENTER

"When you look at the view, the natural instinct would have been to just make a big wall of glass. But the windows actually vary in width, just as when you look at the forest you see trunks of varying width with varying spaces between them. The spirit was to actually connect with the forest itself. [We were trying to make this] direct visual connection."

STEVE CHAITOW

LANDSCAPE FEATURES THAT DEFINE BUILDING FORM: The form of the building is defined by the relationship between the neighborhood on the north side and the stunningly beautiful forest on the south side. The gentle slope of the building's roof promotes rainwater collection, and the Rain Veil provides a unique opportunity for the public to observe and interact with flowing precipitation. The vertical windows on the forest side frame views of the trees and create long shadows across the floors that move with the time of day and seasons. These long, tall windows, with varying widths and alternating bands of vertical black locust wood siding, mimic the forest itself. The building, perched on the edge of the south-facing hill, gives people the unique experience of being suspended in the forest canopy.

EVOLVED HUMAN-NATURE RELATIONSHIPS

EXPLORATION + DISCOVERY: The Center encourages exploration and discovery of the park through interactive features and views that connect visitors with the surrounding forest. The thoughtful entry sequence welcomes people into the building, where the public room and decks connect them to the tree canopy. The Falls Ravine installation invites people to explore the path of water as it moves from sky to roof to creek.

CURIOSITY + ENTICEMENT: The Frick Environmental Center was conceived as a learning tool. The building celebrates natural, locally-sourced materials and exposes and highlights systems that treat water and waste. The integration of these sustainable strategies with public art sparks curiosity about natural processes, and visual connections between the building and the forest and raingardens outside invite people to contemplate the greater ecology of Frick Park. Child-sized doors and interactive features send a message to children that this building is for them, too, enticing them to look, listen, and explore.

PROSPECT + REFUGE: The elevated perspective of the Frick Center allows people to feel as if they are perched on the edge of the forested hill, where they can feel protected without having views obscured. The public living room and classrooms at the Center provide a refuge from the elements and offer inspiring places to sit, read, and reflect while enjoying the prospect, or extensive view, of the forest and raingarden below.

> "Through this sequence of features, you're able to experience the amazing-ness of water during a rain event. You can take it all in—you can hear it, you can see it, you can feel it."
>
> **PATRICIA CULLEY**

> "There's this emotional sequence that takes you from an ordinary sidewalk to a place where you're kind of floating in the forest. By deliberately manipulating where you are in space and by compressing that space, you are drawn to focus on that engagement with nature."
>
> **STEVE CHAITOW**

The tall vertical windows mimic the pattern of trees in the forest.

LIGHT + SPACE

INSIDE-OUTSIDE SPACES: The spine of the building, through which most visitors circulate, is a continuation of the entry and exit bridges at each end, and once inside, people are still connected to the outside through enticing views of the Rain Ravine water sculpture and bridge. The living room feels like a treehouse platform, with full-height windows that blur the lines between wall and forest.

LIGHT + SHADOW: The striking vertical pattern of windows on the forest side of the building casts a playful dance of light and shadow across the spaces and mimics the rhythm of the tree trunks beyond. The south-facing orientation ensures that these shadows change throughout the day and across the year, marking time and season.

SPATIAL VARIABILITY: The deliberate building orientation facilitates the creation of spaces with varied functions. Learning and group activities take place in the south-facing classrooms. The public gallery is located on the elevated second floor, while private offices are found below. Transition spaces are located on the north side of the building. The quality of light, masterfully used to energize, create movement, and focus attention, corresponds to the function of each space.

The scale of each space is carefully controlled to support its function.

"We designed it to have focused connections. As we're lifting people off the ground — first compressing and then opening up [the spaces] — it allows them to have a more focused engagement, so they don't have to take it all in at once."

PATRICIA CULLEY

BETTY & CLINT JOSEY PAVILION

PART I:
IMMERSED IN PLACE

PROJECT NAME:
BETTY & CLINT
JOSEY PAVILION

BUILDING TYPE:
ENVIRONMENTAL
LEARNING CENTER

LOCATION:
DECATUR, TEXAS

**BUILDING
SQUARE FOOTAGE:**
5,400 SQ. FT.

OWNER:
DIXON WATER
FOUNDATION

ARCHITECT:
LAKE|FLATO
ARCHITECTS

**SUSTAINABILITY
CONSULTANTS:**
LAKE|FLATO
ARCHITECTS

....

SPECIAL THANK YOU TO:

TENNA FLORIAN, PROJECT ARCHITECT, LAKE|FLATO ARCHITECTS

COREY SQUIRE, SUSTAINABILITY CONSULTANT, LAKE|FLATO ARCHITECTS

ROBERT POTTS, FOUNDER/OWNER, DIXON WATER FOUNDATION

PART II: DESIGN PROCESS

Built to further the mission of the Dixon Water Foundation, the Betty & Clint Josey Pavilion educates its visitors, many of them children, on watershed protection through sustainable ranching and the restoration of damaged farmland to native tallgrass prairie.

The design concept evolved in response to the site and local climate and was inspired by a beautifully gnarled heritage Live Oak. The Pavilion was designed to function without active heating or cooling systems yet still remain comfortable most of the year; a key strategy was to orient the building to take advantage of prevailing breezes. Designed in response to the North Texas climate, the educational pavilion completely transitions from an enclosed shelter in the winter to an open-air shade structure in the summer. Three sliding panels on each long side open and close, and the walls are comprised of adjustable wood slats. Visitors are protected from the elements without losing access to daylight, natural ventilation or views.

> "This project was about kids, their experience of place, and establishing a love of place because people aren't going to work to protect the environment unless they love that environment."
>
> **TENNA FLORIAN**

PART III: BUILT EXPERIENCE

The experience of the Josey Pavilion is closely tied to the mission of landscape restoration. Visitors find refuge in the buildings without ever losing sight of prairie and sky. Groups of children sit in circles on the floor or under the Live Oak, in each case protected from the harsh Texas sun. They can hear the wind rustling the prairie grasses without the distracting sound of mechanical air conditioning, and through the simple barnlike structures they feel connected to the region's ranching legacy. In the evening, Clint and Betty Josey themselves enjoy coming to the Pavilion to watch the sunset, while the sound of crickets fills the warm summer night and colors streak the sky.

"The most valuable part of the biophilic design charrette process was when we just sat and listened—I mean, seriously listened."

TENNA FLORIAN

"It's all from the site. The orientation was set; the views were set; the strategies were set, because we knew what we had to do to keep people comfortable in different climates. The design just grew out of the conditions."

COREY SQUIRE

"The prairie is a place that is about two things: the sky, and where the sky and land meet. The building is a very simple, low-slung form that accentuates and frames the horizon. The building form responds to the prairie as a whole and accentuates the beauty of the prairie."

TENNA FLORIAN

"I would encourage folks [building owners] to get outdoors and experience the place. It's one thing to look at a place on a map or think about it abstractly; when you're out there you get a sense of where the sun rises at different times of year, of prevailing winds—lots of things you can't anticipate until you experience them."

ROBERT POTTS

PART IV: BIOPHILIC ELEMENTS + ATTRIBUTES

PLACE-BASED RELATIONSHIPS

SPIRIT OF PLACE: The Josey Pavilion is an expression of place, and it is difficult to imagine this building anywhere else other than the North Texas prairie. The climate can be extreme: temperatures climb above 80 degrees for over five months of the year and dip to 30 degrees for a few months in the winter. The wind is almost always present.

But this building is not sealed off from the outside; it does not rely on air conditioning or electric space heating. Instead, the Josey Pavilion responds to climate, opening up in the summer to create a shaded shelter that takes advantage of cooling breezes. Through these built structures, which protect without shutting out the external environment, people begin to forge connections with this particular place, thereby sowing the seeds of stewardship.

"When you're in this building, in most places you're protected from above; you have your back to the wall and you can see out. It very much mimics a comfortable environment in a prairie or savanna."

COREY SQUIRE

"From previous experience, we knew that a tree is better than anything else in blocking the wind because a tree is about thirty-two percent open. A tree allows a little bit of wind through, but for the most part it pushes the breeze over itself. We emulated a tree by having these wood slat panels on our barn doors that block the wind in the winter."

COREY SQUIRE

CASE STUDY: JOSEY PAVILION | 69

ECOLOGICAL CONNECTION TO PLACE: Because the Dixon Water Foundation's mission is to educate visitors about sustainable ranching through grassland restoration, the building owner wanted to create a building that would connect people to the prairie. Naturally, such an educational space should complement the prairie landscape and never lose sight of it.

Far from monotonous, the prairie is dynamic, with ever-changing colors and textures that mark the seasons. The horizon—the strong line joining earth and sky—is the prairie's defining element. The buildings' long, low, and simple forms emulate this horizontal landscape, while the open walls frame the expansive views. Like the Live Oak, the buildings provide a refuge from the elements without alienating people from the landscape. The simple, unfinished materials — wood, rusted steel, and raw concrete— complement the russet, gold, and pale green hues of the prairie grasses and the dramatic cloudscapes.

LANDSCAPE ORIENTATION THAT DEFINES FORM: The buildings are oriented with their long sides facing south and north. Overhangs allow the sun to penetrate the spaces in winter but shade them in summer. Generous verandas line the building, providing shade and a transition space between inside and outside. The heritage oak tree, located in the courtyard adjacent to the two buildings, anchors the structures and provides a natural gathering place.

LIGHT + SPACE

LIGHT + SHADOW:
The slatted walls emulate the openness of a tree canopy, blocking the wind while casting patterned shadows on interior walls and floors. As these shadows move and change, they help create a sense of time, connecting people to the weather and seasons and syncing with the body's circadian rhythms.

SPATIAL VARIABILITY:
Despite its apparent simplicity, the dynamic design of the educational pavilion gives visitors a varied spatial and visual experience. As the slats open and close, the interior is bathed in gradations of light; the building morphs into a transparent form upon which the roof appears to almost float. In contrast, the more solid form of the administrative building grounds the structure in its prairie setting.

The buildings' design and orientation also encourage varying experience of scale. Visitors can focus on the interior courtyard or on the distant horizon, and the building provides "frames" that draw the eye.

INSIDE-OUTSIDE SPACES: The tallgrass prairie is a place of plentiful sunshine, with few places in which to take refuge. In response, the buildings protect occupied spaces from summer heat gain. Overhanging roofs, rolling shutters, and clerestory windows block and filter sunlight and capture the movement of light as the sun tracks across the sky. This movement of light, combined with the simple forms and organic materials palette, helps to define these spaces.

The educational pavilion's design breaks down the barriers between inside and outside. The walls can open up entirely, creating an open-air pavilion, and the verandas provide shaded spaces for people to gather, protected from sun and wind.

NATURAL PATTERNS + PROCESSES

SENSORY VARIABILITY:
Without the distractions of the built environment, those who visit the Josey Pavilion are immersed in the experience of the prairie. Everywhere they look they notice patterns and textures, from the wood grain on the exposed timbers to the constantly shifting clouds. They feel the constant breeze. They enjoy the sweet fragrance of the grasses and the warmth of the direct sunlight on their skin; they listen to the sounds of wind caressing the grasses and rustling the leaves of the oak tree and the roll of distant thunder. They hear the song of the meadowlark, the clicking of grasshoppers, and the soft drone of crickets and other insects. The richness and variety of this sensory stimulation evokes memories and stirs emotions and helps ground people in this very specific and special place.

TRANSITIONAL SPACES:
The Josey Pavilion provides several places from which to transition from the built environment to the natural prairie. The educational building is a beautiful example of a structure that itself transforms from an enclosed room to an open-air pavilion, modulating the degree of exposure to outside conditions. Similarly, the verandas between buildings provide spaces that are not quite indoors but not quite outdoors, either—protected places from which people can enjoy the views and breezes without being completely exposed. The courtyard, sheltered as it is by the heritage oak tree and the buildings, serves as a transitional place between the buildings and the open prairie.

R.W. KERN CENTER

PART I: CENTERED ON NATURE

PROJECT NAME:
R.W. KERN CENTER

BUILDING TYPE:
EDUCATIONAL

LOCATION:
AMHERST, MASSACHUSETTS

BUILDING SQUARE FOOTAGE:
17,000 SQ. FT.

OWNER:
HAMPSHIRE COLLEGE

CONSTRUCTION MANAGEMENT:
WRIGHT BUILDERS INC

ARCHITECT:
BRUNER/COTT ARCHITECTS AND PLANNERS

LANDSCAPE ARCHITECT:
RICHARD BURKE ASSOCIATES

ENGINEER (SITE/CIVIL AND PERMITTING):
BERKSHIRE DESIGN GROUP

SPECIAL THANK YOU TO:

JONATHAN WRIGHT, CONSTRUCTION MANAGER, WRIGHT BUILDERS INC

JASON FORNEY, ARCHITECT, BRUNER/COTT ARCHITECTS AND PLANNERS

JASON JEWHURST, ARCHITECT, BRUNER/COTT ARCHITECTS AND PLANNERS

Large or small, every space in the building celebrates the beautiful rural setting.

> "When we were setting goals for the project, one of the things that came up over and over again was the natural beauty of the natural setting in which our building was sited—the mountains and hills—the views are panoramic. We thought we really had to take advantage of those views and vistas. We framed a lot of those views, even by the way we oriented the building."
>
> **JASON FORNEY**

> "You don't really know if these solid forms [the two wings of the building] are crushing into the glass piece [atrium] and pushing it out, or pulling away from it, enlarging it and making it more open. What I experience in the way these forms interact is the sense of a slow evolutionary process happening."
>
> **JONATHAN WRIGHT**

PART II: DESIGN PROCESS

The R.W. Kern Center, prominently sited on the campus of Hampshire College, serves as a welcome center for staff, students, and their families and the central meeting point for the campus community. As an embodiment of the values of Hampshire College, the Center sends a strong sustainability message to students, staff and visitors.

The design team incorporated biophilic design elements deliberately, using Kellert's framework to identify specific attributes early in the process. The commitment to biophilic design was maintained from design through construction with regular workshops that included both the design team and the faculty and staff, and students who would ultimately call the Kern Center their own.

A central design driver was to celebrate the project's context, a rural setting that includes inspiring views of the Holyoke Range. The building form, consisting of a central atrium from which two stone-clad wings emerge, was oriented to preserve and highlight these views. With a common area, community living room, and café on the ground floor and gallery above, the two-story glass atrium maintains a connection to the outdoors and serves as a hub of campus activity, while the wings house administrative offices and classrooms.

PART III: BUILT EXPERIENCE

The R.W. Kern Center provides a much-needed heart for the Hampshire College campus—a place to welcome prospective and current students. The Center translates the identity of Hampshire College into a built form that communicates the college's values and unique approach to education.

Entering the building through its main entry, visitors find themselves in a light-filled, two-story commons. Prospective students begin their tour of the campus on the second floor, where large windows frame views of the hills, meadows, and woods, which turn a patchwork of green, russet, and yellow in autumn.

Students and faculty alike can find a quiet corner or join the bustling atmosphere of the café. Many take a moment to enjoy a moment of calm relaxation and appreciate the beauty of the setting. Students who have a little more time explore the curious numbers, letters, shapes, and other markings embedded in many of the interior features.

PART IV: BIOPHILIC ELEMENTS + ATTRIBUTES

ENVIRONMENTAL FEATURES

NATURAL MATERIALS: Dominated by stone, wood, and glass, the Kern Center was built using a simple palette of local materials that are left largely unfinished and exposed. The distinctive Ashfield mica-schist stone that is used both externally and internally was extracted from a small quarry only twenty-five miles away and delivered to the site in small batches.

Stacked on the façades of the two "wings," the stone layers evoke the geomorphic strata in natural formations. The warm gray-blue tones, rich sheen, and ridged patterning of the stone complements the bands of concrete and horizontal wood cladding. Inside the building, the aggregates are exposed in the diamond-polished concrete floor. These materials, unpainted and minimally finished, celebrate the work of human hands and evoke a sense of reverence and affection for the building and the place from which it comes.

HABITATS + ECOSYSTEMS: Planted beds run along the south-facing wall. Not only do these plants provide pleasing greenery for the atrium, they treat greywater from all sinks in the building and create natural habitat. Given the cold climate in winter, the plants provide a welcome green buffer when snow is on the ground. The planted beds also help students understand how plant roots and bacteria treat wastewater naturally by extracting and consuming nutrients.

VIEWS + VISTAS: The R.W. Kern Center's location was deliberately chosen to orient future students on tours of Hampshire College, helping them comprehend the campus layout and appreciate the beauty of the rural location. The building is oriented to celebrate significant views, and the design uses windows and large openings to frame and emphasize a hierarchy of these views. The south-facing central common area highlights expansive vistas of the Holyoke Range and The Notch, a prominent local landmark, while offices and classrooms offer glimpses of the amphitheater, rainwater harvesting reservoirs, solar farm, and wildflower meadow.

"We started out by taking the whole of Kellert's framework and tried to narrow down the attributes, not for the sake of making it easier, but so that we could connect more clearly to a smaller number of them."

JASON FORNEY

"The collaboration that the Living Building work requires—because nobody has all the answers—means that there is a good deal of listening and collaboration. So right away, there is a coevolution that happens among the people in the team, which reflects what nature does."

JONATHAN WRIGHT

"By the end of schematic design we had two or three attributes in each category that we thought we were applying. As we moved forward, the ones that were most in our hearts and minds got more and more connected to the actual project."

JASON FORNEY

CASE STUDY: R.W. KERN CENTER | 79

The distinctive mica-schist stone grounds the building in its place.

"From day one, we were focused on making sure that every single material and every surface that you could encounter in the building was connected to the culture of the region."

JASON JEWHURST

"The process of making the building [involved] finding things in our own backyard, and that created a kind of exploration to get off the internet and into the outdoors."

JONATHAN WRIGHT

"The masons who worked with the stones treated them like they were precious objects. When you have that strong connection of care and craft, people get to experience it when they come into the space."

JASON JEWHURST

NATURAL PATTERNS + PROCESSES

CENTRAL FOCAL POINT: The two-story glazed atrium serves as the R.W. Kern Center's heart. In contrast with the solid forms and more enclosed spaces of the office and classroom wings, this central common space is open and energetic, with expansive views out to the campus and landscape beyond. With puzzles incorporated into the interior materials, a second-floor overlook, quiet corners, and bustling café seating, the atrium provides a variety of experiences, as well a place where people can gather.

In a broader sense, as the gateway into campus from the north, the Kern Center serves as a central focal point for pedestrian traffic, introducing visitors to culture of Hampshire College along the way.

LINKED SERIES + CHAINS: The atrium serves as a hub, linking the two wings of the building to this central point. From this public common area, the building's more private program elements branch off. Progressing from the atrium into each wing, the orientation, views, and light all change, scaling down from open and expansive to more intimate and enclosed.

The building itself also serves as a hub and vital link to other parts of the campus. Several footpaths intersect at the building, and views through the glazed atrium reinforce the link between the northern outer campus and central quad.

INFORMATION RICHNESS: In addition to the sensory stimulation that comes with the interplay of materials, light, and views, ten puzzles are embedded into the building. A series of letters emblazoned on the underside of stair treads; a curious pattern of light and dark squares and rectangles inlaid into a floor board near a bench; a pattern of red and white painted pipe clamps high on the ceiling—these puzzles draw attention to aspects of the building people might otherwise not notice, inviting the visitor to pause and look more closely while contemplating the puzzles' meanings.

"We designed this building with two wings that were more opaque in the center. You always felt that there was this focal point that helps you feel comfortable; you can sense it from inside and outside."
JASON FORNEY

"When we go to see a dance performance and the dancer makes a gesture, we experience something: maybe birdlike, maybe froglike—something that's not actually there. Buildings that are in touch with their locations—those that have been invested with heart by the people who design and make them—do that. They're dynamic, living things."
JONATHAN WRIGHT

"We know that the light changes from orange-yellow back to purple and blue. How the spaces react, how the materials absorb some of these colors from the environment creates a richness that we're seeing as the different seasons unfold in the building."

JASON JEWHURST

LIGHT + SPACE

NATURAL LIGHT: The building's shallow width and passive solar orientation allow every space to be flooded with natural light. In the two-story atrium, open expanses of glass create a visual connection through the building. The atrium gathers light and distributes it to adjacent spaces, while open layouts help occupants maintain a connection to the outdoors from wherever they are inside the building.

LIGHT + SHADOW: The dramatic south-facing glazed wall allows sunlight to penetrate deep into the space, creating shadows that change during the day and throughout each season. The exposed wood beams and concrete floor of the atrium reflect the changing sun angle with colors that shift and deepen.

SPACIOUSNESS: The high ceilings and proportion of glazing in the atrium creates a sense of spaciousness, where the walls disappear and the ceiling seems to float above. The transparent staircases and open layout enhance the open, lofty quality.

CASE STUDY: R.W. KERN CENTER | 85

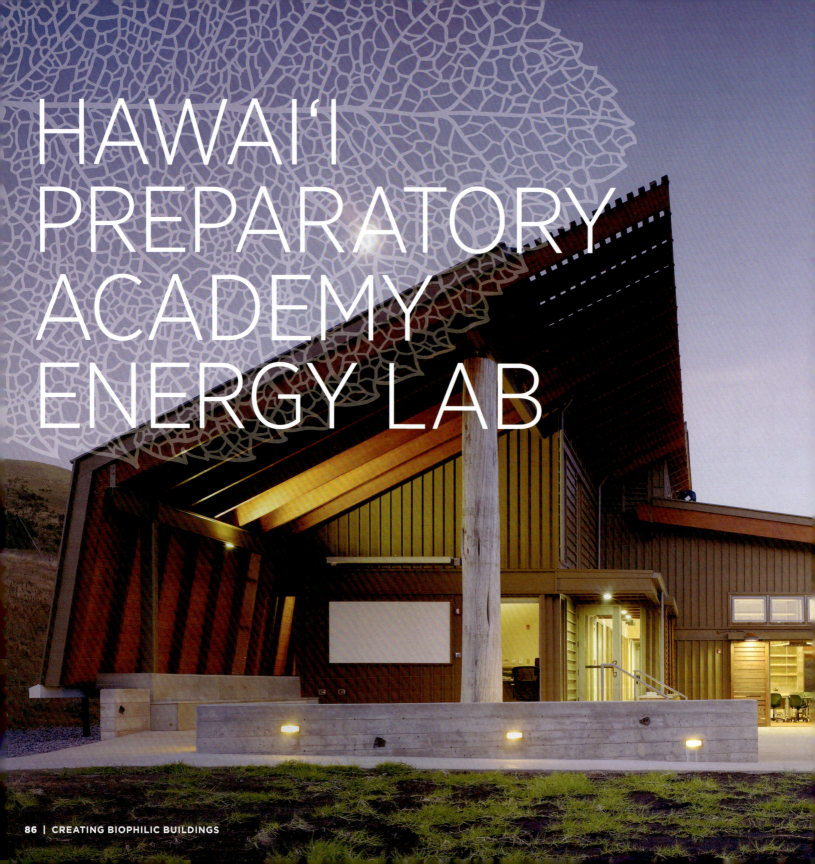

PART I: RESPONDING TO WIND, SUN, AND SEA

PROJECT NAME:
HAWAI'I PREPARATORY
ACADEMY ENERGY LAB

BUILDING TYPE:
EDUCATIONAL

LOCATION:
KAMUELA, HAWAI'I

BUILDING SQUARE FOOTAGE:
5,902 SQ. FT.

OWNER:
HAWAI'I PREPARATORY
ACADEMY

ARCHITECT:
FLANSBURGH
ARCHITECTS

LANDSCAPE ARCHITECT:
KEN AND RMG

SUSTAINABILITY CONSULTANT:
BURO HAPPOLD,
SUSTAINABILITY
AND LEED QUALITY
BUILDERS INC.

SPECIAL THANK YOU TO:

BILL WIECKING, ENERGY LAB DIRECTOR & OWNER'S REPRESENTATIVE, HPA

DAVID CROTEAU, PROJECT ARCHITECT, FLANSBURGH ARCHITECTS

PART II: DESIGN PROCESS

Located in Kamuela, Hawai'i and set among the rolling foothills of the Kohala Mountains, the Hawai'i Preparatory Academy Energy Lab was created to educate the next generation of students in the understanding of environmentally conscious, sustainable living systems.

The team held several week-long working sessions on the site, an approach that allowed them to study design ideas from multiple perspectives and which fostered systems integration. Energy Lab Director Bill Wiecking encouraged students to participate in the design process while challenging the design team to create spaces they wished to learn in and from.

The challenges of the site were also its greatest assets. The Energy Lab is located in one of the sunniest and windiest places in the country. The design team created a building that connects to this special place while relying solely on natural ventilation and passive cooling. The prevailing north winds defined the dramatically sloped north-facing roof, and the building was oriented to both harness solar power and connect to the stunning views to the south. Extensive physical models and dynamic energy and thermal models helped refine the building shape and placement of windows. More than simply a building that runs on wind and sun, the Energy Lab fosters engaged learning and pays homage to both the land and to Hawaiian culture.

"This project was about understanding and being really sensitive to a particular place."
DAVID CROTEAU

"This is a collaborative learning space; we don't wall off the rooms and make them our little kingdoms."
BILL WIECKING

> "The project sits on a slope, and the inside has three levels that step down the slope, so you feel like you're part of the topography. We were looking for ways that the building could enhance the experience of being on the hill."
>
> **DAVID CROTEAU**

> "The reason that biophilic design was so organic here is because it came out of the fact that we all live here and we know what fits… [The building] fits into the surroundings; it doesn't look like a foreign structure. It's sensitive to the wind, sensitive to the light, sensitive to the views."
>
> **BILL WIECKING**

> "We made the conscious decision to reorient the building toward the view and sacrifice a little bit of the efficiency of the solar panels. That speaks to the importance of nature—the balance of harnessing nature in different ways. You're harnessing the sun for power, but you're giving some of that up to harness the view, which tells you where you are."
>
> **DAVID CROTEAU**

PART III: BUILT EXPERIENCE

When students and visitors enter the Energy Lab at the Hawai'i Preparatory Academy, they do not experience an abrupt transition between outside and inside. Instead, the building protects them from the full force of the wind without cutting them off from surrounding sights and sounds. Skylights and louvered windows allow in filtered and diffused light, and glass doors and windows connect learning and research spaces. In this open and collaborative environment, students can what see other groups are doing and interact with them. The Energy Lab teaches students how architectural design can create and enhance a person's connection to the environment and immerses them in a hands-on exploration of the role buildings play in consuming and generating energy. Students can experiment and interact with the building, learning how climate, winds, and daily temperature impact energy generation and use while comparing its performance to buildings around the world.

PART IV: BIOPHILIC ELEMENTS + ATTRIBUTES

PLACE-BASED RELATIONSHIPS

SPIRIT OF PLACE: The Energy Lab enjoys strong connections to the hillside topography, the stunning views of the valley below, and the 4,000-foot Mauna Kea volcano to the south. The building form is defined by its relationship to climate; the roof pitches, overhangs, and carefully placed openings are a response to site-specific breezes and orientation to the sun. In this way, the building blends elements of traditional huts, which use southern porches, or lanai, to funnel cooling breezes inside, with the best of today's technologies. Such an approach captures the spirit of Hawai'i, where people enjoy a strong connection to the land, water, and beauty of their island home.

ECOLOGICAL CONNECTION TO PLACE: Like the other Hawaiian Islands, the Big Island experiences many different microclimates. On the island's north side, daytime temperatures hover in the 80s all year round, but strong trade winds and cooler nights are common. The lab connects to the ecology of place by utilizing the sun and wind to drive the form and functions of the building. By generating all of the energy it needs through solar energy, harnessing the wind for natural ventilation, and collecting rainwater and treating it onsite, the building does not diminish the ecological functions of its surroundings, but instead fosters an attitude of respect and appreciation for natural systems.

LANDSCAPE ORIENTATION: The Energy Lab was designed in response to this particular place in the Hawaiian landscape. The stepped arrangement of building components reflects the hillside topography, and the building was sited to best take advantage of the prevailing breezes from the north. The passive strategies for cooling the building depend on building orientation and form. The sharply angled north-facing roof directs most of the strong trade winds up and over the building, while louvers allow in just enough air to facilitate natural ventilation.

The transparent nature of the classrooms reflects the collaborative spirit of research.

LIGHT + SPACE

FILTERED + DIFFUSED LIGHT: The light outside the Energy Lab is bright and vivid. The building form skillfully controls this light without isolating occupants from the sun's path across the sky; consequently, people inside the building feel as if they are under the protection of a shade tree. Translucent skylights, wooden sunscreens, and interior roller shades work together to manage daylight, washing rooms in diffused light and casting dappled shadows while protecting the interior from solar heat gain.

LIGHT AS SHAPE + FORM: The building form itself was shaped by the quality and quantity of light falling on this sunny, exposed hillside, and the building's roofs are designed to control and direct light as well as minimize solar heat gain. But in addition to these practical functions, the skylights and louvers use light as a medium, creating dynamic sculptural shapes that fill the vaulted spaces and shift and change throughout the day.

INSIDE-OUTSIDE SPACES: In the beautiful climate of Hawai'i, living outside is a way of life. The Energy Lab pays homage to this lifestyle with outdoor classrooms and indoor classrooms that feel like they are outside. Glass doors enhance the connection to the outdoors, and sheltered porches and entries blur the lines between inside and outside. Skylights and windows bring views and light into spaces, and the building successfully balances the need to maintain temperatures conducive to studying and researching with the psychological benefits of daylight and immersion in the beauty of place.

CASE STUDY: HAWAI'I PREPARATORY ACADEMY ENERGY LAB

Deceptively simple in appearance, the building form is attuned to the sun and wind in this particular location.

EVOLVED HUMAN-NATURE RELATIONSHIPS

SECURITY + PROTECTION: The windy, exposed site leaves people vulnerable to direct sunlight, heat, and constant wind. The Energy Lab protects occupants from overexposure to these elements and fosters a healthy, inspiring atmosphere for learning and discovery, enhanced by natural light, fresh air, and expansive views.

ORDER + COMPLEXITY: The building form is simple, composed of sloping roofs and rectangular spaces. The floorplan arranges these spaces in a logical and orderly fashion, while at the same time the scale of each varies and presents the visitor with changing views and perspectives. The building juxtaposes a simple palette of materials—glass, concrete, and wood—with complex patterns of light and line. The wood louvers allow in slatted shafts of light, echoed in the longitudinal pattern of planking on the building's façade and interior ceiling, while windows and skylights wash the spaces with softer, diffused sunlight.

ATTRACTION + BEAUTY: The beauty of this building lies in the combination of the elegant scale of each space and the articulation of the materials that frame them. The simplicity of the building's overall form belies the complexity of thought and modeling that went into perfecting it, and like a bird's wing, there is beauty in a form that so obviously describes its function. There is beauty in the contrast between the rich, warm wood and the simple raw concrete, and these organic materials complement the rolling hills, open sky, and ocean backdrop. The building openings frame distant views, creating a sense of tranquility and connection to water and sky, while the stepped forms root into the hillside.

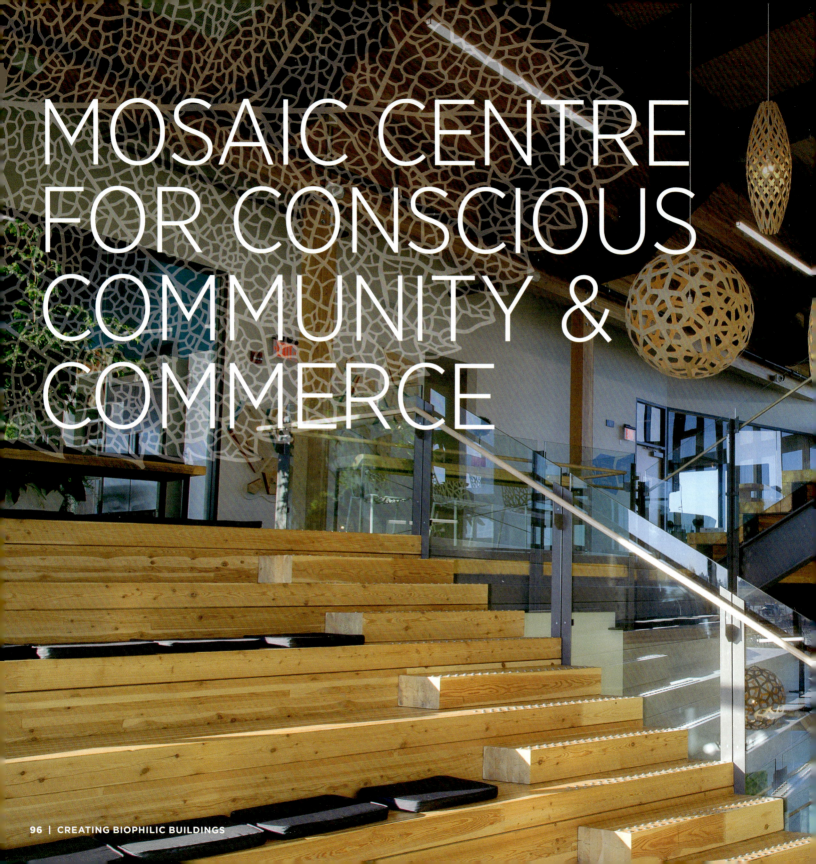

MOSAIC CENTRE FOR CONSCIOUS COMMUNITY & COMMERCE

PART I:
CREATING COMMUNITY

PROJECT NAME:
MOSAIC CENTRE FOR CONSCIOUS COMMUNITY AND COMMERCE

BUILDING TYPE:
COMMERCIAL/ EDUCATIONAL

LOCATION:
EDMONTON, ALBERTA, CANADA

BUILDING SQUARE FOOTAGE:
30,000 SQ. FT.

OWNERS:
DENNIS CUKU & CHRISTY BENOIT

ARCHITECT:
MANASC ISAAC ARCHITECTS

SUSTAINABILITY CONSULTANTS:
ECOAMMO SUSTAINABLE CONSULTING

SPECIAL THANK YOU TO:

DENNIS CUKU, OWNER

VEDRAN SKOPAC, PROJECT ARCHITECT, MANASC ISAAC ARCHITECTS

STEPHANI CARTER, SUSTAINABILITY CONSULTANT, ECOAMMO SUSTAINABLE CONSULTING

PART II: DESIGN PROCESS

As its name implies, the Mosaic Centre for Conscious Community and Commerce is much more than commercial office space, but rather is a re-imagining of the work environment as a rejuvenating space that fosters collaboration, creativity, and well-being.

Project owners Dennis Cuku and Christy Benoit began the design process by creating a "project manifesto" with sustainability consultant Stephani Carter. The declaration describes the vision of a future sustainable community and includes a design story and a "wish list" of desired outcomes. Utilizing an Integrated Project Delivery (IPD) process, the design team sought to create a building that promotes interactions among people and between people, architecture, and nature.

Located in Summerside, a community in south Edmonton, Alberta, the 30,000-square-foot building includes a restaurant, childcare center, wellness center, and co-working office spaces. A central atrium brings all of these elements together. More than simply a transition space, the atrium includes nooks and places that invite people to linger and is the heart of the building.

98 | CREATING BIOPHILIC BUILDINGS

"We very much understood that if we were to be successful in this project, we had to create more of a feeling instead of a mechanical place. We needed not just spaces, but something that people could belong to."
DENNIS CUKU

"The hope is that this building will help create a culture that will inspire each individual and group to release the creativity that is oppressed somewhere deep down inside in our linear and conformant lives, and last but not least, tolerate the errors and imperfections made along the way."
VEDRAN SKOPAC

"We spent a lot of time making sure that the spaces felt right. [This] feeling good actually has to do with space size, geometrical proportions, how much privacy is appropriate, and these other elements that are hard to quantify."
DENNIS CUKU

PART III: BUILT EXPERIENCE

As Project Architect Vedran Skopac describes it, the Mosaic Centre was designed to emulate a rich and colorful city with an intimacy and familiarity of a tiny house. People coming to use the building do not necessarily head straight for a desk and get to work; instead, the layout promotes unplanned "collisions" and interactions, so that a person is just as likely to become engrossed in an exciting conversation or find themselves on the terrace, contemplating the "village" of greenhouses atop the roof. They may also end up on the atrium bleachers, where they can take advantage of the abundant natural light and enjoy the stimulating collage of crisscrossing stairways, intricate light fixtures, and wall of greenery. Whether working quietly alone or engaged with others, the Centre provides a creative and collaborative working space for innovation.

"… we need to make a very conscious choice to move into designing spaces that do support the human experience. At the very heart of it, if all of us were to follow what was natural, we would design spaces like [the Mosaic Centre]. It really came down to getting the team to get in touch with what felt most natural, and then finding a way to incorporate that into the design."

DENNIS CUKU

Much more than a workspace, the Mosaic Centre also includes a restaurant which uses produce cultivated on the site.

"We also rotated the building to find the optimal angle. This also created a more intimate environment on the southeast corner of the site. Pushing the building away from the westbound road created a deeper green space with terraces around the building, which benefits from the [standpoint of] passive solar design, but which also created more human conditions on the site."

VEDRAN SKOPAC

"From the beginning and in that manifesto we had the green wall, the atrium, and the stairwells that go up and down with different angles. There's so much that the client wanted [to include in order to create] that sense of place that we were able to execute in the project. I really attribute that to changing the design process."

STEPHANI CARTER

PART IV: BIOPHILIC ELEMENTS + ATTRIBUTES

LIGHT + SPACE

NATURAL LIGHT: The building was designed with a narrow cross-section and is aligned along the east-west axis, ensuring every space benefits from daylighting. Large sections of uninterrupted glazing allow in abundant natural light, both in the central atrium and in the spaces surrounding it. Many of the connected spaces are separated by glass partitions rather than solid walls, borrowing light from the central atrium and fostering a sense of openness and collaboration.

LIGHT + SHADOW: Light and shadow animate the atrium, creating sunny gathering spaces that contrast with constantly moving shadows that connect occupants with the season and time of day. Because the building relies primarily on natural lighting, there is considerable variability in the illumination of spaces, much as a forest is characterized by light and shadowed areas. The light fixtures also play with light, as light coming in through the cutout shapes highlights their intricate structure. All of these patterns create a sense of mystery and dynamism that stimulates creativity.

SPACIOUSNESS: The central atrium is three stories tall. Visitors experience this sun-filled volume as soon as they enter the building. The space is activated by David Trubridge's dynamic lights and enhanced by the glass-lined staircases, which draw the eye ever upward. In contrast, smaller, more intimate spaces radiate out from this large, open volume.

"We wanted to maximize the solar exposure, so we elongated the building east to west and created the least wide cross-section, so we have the highest amount of natural daylight and the least amount of artificial light"

VEDRAN SKOPAC

The spacious atrium is a stimulating space where welcome "collisions" occur.

NATURAL PATTERNS + PROCESSES

CENTRAL FOCAL POINT: The Mosaic Centre is organized with more private spaces toward the east and west and group spaces toward the interior. Every space faces onto the very public atrium. With bleacher-style seating that invites occupants to sit, work, and gather, the atrium is the heart of the Center, connecting all spaces to and through it and providing the sense of community and connectedness that the owners were striving for. The green wall provides a vertical connection up through all three stories.

SENSORY VARIABILITY: From the moment people step inside, this building engages the senses. In the atrium, occupants notice the pleasant sound of people conversing and the rhythm of footsteps on the wooden staircases; they feel the change in humidity near the green wall and the alternating patterns of warmth and cool corresponding to light and shadow. Their eyes are drawn to the contrasting angles of the transparent staircases; the texture of wood grain and plant leaves; and the light fixtures' intriguing geometry. In contrast, the office and childcare spaces are quiet and simple, facilitating creative work and play.

FRACTALS: Fractals are complex patterns that rely on the repetition of simple shapes. Though they exist all around us, from the microbial to cosmic scales, they are rarely used in building design. David Trubridge has been inspired by fractals since he was a child, and his light fixtures draw inspiration from snowflakes, woven baskets, and geometric polyhedra. While his lights are beautiful, they also connect building occupants to the shapes and patterns so ubiquitous in nature.

> "The green wall is a main focus; it's the largest feature in the building, and you can see it from outside of the building. It adds greenery and color in the building, but it also adds humidity and a kind of a feeling to the space."
>
> **STEPHANI CARTER**

CASE STUDY: MOSAIC CENTRE FOR CONSCIOUS COMMUNITY AND COMMERCE

EVOLVED HUMAN-NATURE RELATIONSHIPS

"The intention from the owners was to have a community building where people come in and feel like it's their own. That's part of why there's this openness to it, and the interesting design makes it inviting—you want to go and climb up those stairs."

STEPHANI CARTER

PROSPECT + REFUGE: The central atrium provides a place where the whole building and those moving within it can be taken in; at the same time, it provides elevated views of the surrounding suburban environment. Occupants can take shelter in the many nooks scattered throughout the atrium, whether sitting at a desk on the bleachers, surrounded by a protective cover of plants, or at a workstation on one of the landings, where a person can work alone but still enjoy both the activity of the atrium and the views through the windows.

CURIOSITY + ENTICEMENT: The type and arrangement of spaces in the building cultivates an environment of creativity and curiosity. With the underlying assumption that surprise and playfulness are important ingredients in a productive and vibrant workplace, the building, and in particular, the open atrium, were designed to encourage interactions. People can work or sit in unconventional places, such as the bleacher staircase, and the dynamic design encourages people to linger and explore. The vertical green wall, stimulating light fixtures, and transparent staircases pull visitors upward, their urge to discover spurring their movement through the space.

ORDER + COMPLEXITY: The Mosaic Centre is composed of a simple palette of materials and orderly shapes, lines, and forms; at the same time, complex and contrasting patterns create a stimulating and varied environment, similar to that found in many natural settings. A Fibonacci spiral is integrated into the green wall, and public plazas on the north and south sides of the building and the floor plans and elevations are grounded in the golden mean. These geometric principles create both order and complexity in the interior, allowing occupants to simultaneously lose themselves in the design while remaining oriented in the building.

"The Mosaic Centre was designed to strike a balance between order and complexity — to stimulate the desire for variety, but in ways that seem controlled and comprehensible. For example, the basic layout of spaces, both public and private, is quickly understood by inhabitants because most spaces are large and open and people can readily see from one space to many others. However, there is a pleasing complexity to the spaces due to the irregular rotated dual grid system that encourages non-right angles."

**ROBERT THORTON,
MANASC ISAAC ARCHITECTS**

"The Mosaic Centre conveys strong feelings of protection from threatening forces in nature. The structure is composed of substantial solid wood elements that feel strong and supportive in spaces both large and small, public and private. Although it is located in a region with extreme northern climate, which may be observed through the windows, the high-performance triple-pane glazing and warm-to-the-touch, non-conductive framing engenders feelings of security and protection without isolating occupants from the outside world."

**ROBERT THORTON,
MANASC ISAAC ARCHITECTS**

VANDUSEN BOTANICAL GARDEN VISITOR CENTRE

PART I:
A FLOWER IN THE GARDEN

PROJECT NAME:
VANDUSEN BOTANICAL GARDEN VISITOR CENTRE

BUILDING TYPE:
VISITOR CENTER

LOCATION:
VANCOUVER, BRITISH COLUMBIA, CANADA

BUILDING SQUARE FOOTAGE:
19,000 SQ. FT.

OWNER:
VANCOUVER BOARD OF PARKS AND RECREATION

ARCHITECT:
PERKINS+WILL

LANDSCAPE ARCHITECT:
CONNECT LANDSCAPE (PREVIOUSLY SHAP & DIAMOND LANDSCAPE ARCHITECTURE INC.) WITH CORNELIA HAHN OBERLANDER

SUSTAINABILITY CONSULTANT:
PERKINS+WILL

SPECIAL THANK YOU TO:

JOHN ROSS, PROJECT MANAGER/OWNER'S REPRESENTATIVE, CITY OF VANCOUVER

PETER BUSBY, DESIGN PARTNER, PERKINS+WILL

KATHY WARDLE, SUSTAINABLE DESIGN EXPERT, PERKINS+WILL

KEN LARSSON, LANDSCAPE ARCHITECT, CONNECT LANDSCAPE

PART II: DESIGN PROCESS

Built to increase visitorship and to promote human-nature interactions, the VanDusen Botanical Garden Visitor Centre serves as the hub for a mature 55-acre botanical garden located in the heart of Vancouver, British Columbia. The Center includes a café, an expanded library, volunteer facilities, a garden shop, office space, and flexible classroom spaces. Through a charrette process that included all of the key players, including an ecologist, the design team strove to create a building that is at once iconic and that also integrates harmoniously into the surrounding landscape. The team looked to natural forms for guidance. The overall building form was inspired by the White Bog Orchid, a small and lovely flower that thrives in streamside and wetland settings across much of Canada. Undulating vegetated roof "petals" seem to float above glass windows and curving walls made from rammed earth and concrete. The petals converge to a central skylight oculus, which washes the space in natural light and facilitates natural ventilation. Land ramps link the roof petals to the ground plane, inviting local fauna to access the habitat.

> "The City and Parks Board saw this as an opportunity to renew a civic landmark and a center for public education, and they really wanted the Centre to be an inspiration to connect its visitors with the natural landscape."
>
> **KATHY WARDLE**

The ribbed roof "petals" and central skylight oculus bring a dramatic beauty to the building's interior.

CASE STUDY: VANDUSEN BOTANICAL GARDEN VISITOR CENTRE

"We literally designed the architecture and landscape continuously together; in so doing, they are very interwoven—and that's the way we wanted it. We wanted the building and the landscape and nature to be one."

PETER BUSBY

"Part of making biophilic design successful is taking the opportunity to walk the site and look at the natural features and understand how the building can either restore something that was once there or enhance what is there and understand how the building can contribute and work within the natural ecological setting. Most people find this challenging because it is not something that has been central to design discussions."

KATHY WARDLE

The rammed-earth walls echo the undulating roof petals.

PART III: BUILT EXPERIENCE

Two rammed-earth walls on the east side of the building welcome visitors as they approach, drawing them into the building. Once inside, visitors are compelled to the building's literal center, where an oculus skylight high above draws fresh air and natural light into the space. In this lofty atrium, visitors can look up and appreciate the warm, curving pattern of wood or look through the transparent walls out into the gardens beyond. From the atrium, visitors can exit into the gardens or access the building's many amenities.

CASE STUDY: VANDUSEN BOTANICAL GARDEN VISITOR CENTRE

PART IV: BIOPHILIC ELEMENTS + ATTRIBUTES

NATURAL SHAPES + FORMS

SHAPES RESISTING STRAIGHT LINES + RIGHT ANGLES: Like the orchid it emulates, the Visitor Centre has few straight lines or right angles. The six sections of the roof mimic the complex geometry of flower petals, and these undulating shapes are echoed in the sinuous rammed earth walls. Within the walls, variegated earth-toned bands evoke natural geologic strata. When inside the Centre, the undulating ceilings and curved walls create a multi-dimensional experience that connects people to the natural forms of the plants in the garden beyond the building. The curving lines seem to flow with movement, simultaneously drawing people to the building's light-filled center and expanding outward into the surrounding garden landscape.

SIMULATION OF NATURAL FEATURES: With its asymmetrical vegetated roofs, the Visitor Centre seems of the landscape. The roof structure abstractly simulates a flower, giving visitors the sense of being contained within a natural form. When inside, the wood slatted ceiling evoke the gills of a mushroom. The form of the building hints at its functions—gathering light and rain and attracting visitors—just as a flower draws pollinators and a curved leaf funnels water.

BIOMIMICRY: A beautiful and dramatic focal point where all the roof "petals" converge, the central skylight oculus also serves a practical function: to cool the building and facilitate natural ventilation. Its form was inspired by the genius of the termite mound, which uses an earthen chimney to expel heat and cool the inside. Similarly, hot air rises and vents out through operable windows in the oculus, drawing in cooler air from below. A perforated aluminum suncatcher heightens the stack effect by creating a greater temperature differential between the oculus and the floor level.

White Bog Orchid at Calaveras Big Trees State Park, California, USA

The roof petals create "land ramps" that allow coyotes, foxes and other animals to access the rooftop habitat.

CASE STUDY: VANDUSEN BOTANICAL GARDEN VISITOR CENTRE

PLACE-BASED RELATIONSHIPS

LANDSCAPE FEATURES THAT DEFINE BUILDING FORM: The botanical garden context defines the form of the Visitor Centre, which is set into the landscape like a woodland flower. The roof "petals" connect to grade via vegetated paths so that the transition from garden to roof is seamless, and it is difficult to distinguish where the building ends and garden begins. With its many windows, the building itself is transparent, so that people can see through it to the gardens no matter where they are.

INDIGENOUS MATERIALS: The simple palette of materials and organic shapes help the Visitor Centre seem of the site. The rammed earth walls are built using local soils, and the varying bands of earth-tone pigmentation in these walls connects people to a sense of geology and to the earth on which they stand. The project is constructed largely out of wood, an abundant resource in the Pacific Northwest. Inside and out, the rich, warm tones of the timbers and cladding connect visitors to the region's forests and ground the building in place.

INTEGRATION OF CULTURE + ECOLOGY: The Visitor Centre cultivates a rich environment for all—from people and plants to pollinators and predators. The Centre was created to excite, educate, and inspire visitors about the world of plants, and the unique and nature-inspired building serves as a transition space for people visiting from the city, readying them for the plants in the botanical garden, which is itself a product of human culture. The project included a streamside restoration, and the building's green roofs were designed to attract and support native fauna. Specific areas include native plants that support butterfly colonies, and literal physical connections encourage creatures—even coyotes—to access the roof ecosystem.

"We made the building as transparent as possible, so when you're approaching the building you can see through it and see nature everywhere from within it; you feel like you're still part of nature when you're in the building."

PETER BUSBY

> "The exposed timber structure inside is warm and interesting; people look up at the ceiling and are intrigued by it as an architectural element. It kind of swoops you into the building, and then in the center, there's this oculus, which really draws your attention. There's a lot of curiosity about how all of these elements come together."
>
> **KATHY WARDLE**

EVOLVED HUMAN-NATURE RELATIONSHIPS

The skylight oculus and unusual building form arouse visitors' curiosity.

CURIOSITY + ENTICEMENT:
At once unusual yet somehow familiar, the natural form of the building stimulates wonder, inviting people to explore it and puzzle over its structure. The slatted petals converge in the central oculus, drawing the eye to a feature which is both beautiful and practical. The complex geometry sparks curiosity about its underlying structure and the multiple functions it supports.

REVERENCE + SPIRITUALITY:
Like shafts of light through stained glass, the oculus casts an ever-changing pool of light on the floor below, prompting people to pause and reflect. The lofty, light-filled atrium serves as a central focal point which uses the alchemy of light to transform ordinary materials into something more, indicating that this is a special place worthy of care and respect.

ATTRACTION + BEAUTY:
Just as people are attracted to the delicate but purposeful structure of the orchid, so they are attracted to the beauty of this building. The curved forms, organic colors, and pleasing patterns resonate with people in the same way as do flowers, forests, and rolling hills.

"The thing that seems to attract the most attention is the central oculus, which has a solar chimney and skylight. People always stop there and wonder what the heck is going on."

JOHN ROSS

CASE STUDY: VANDUSEN BOTANICAL GARDEN VISITOR CENTRE

DAVID & LUCILE PACKARD FOUNDATION

PART I:
EMBRACING CLIMATE

PROJECT NAME:
DAVID & LUCILE PACKARD FOUNDATION

BUILDING TYPE:
OFFICE

LOCATION:
LOS ALTOS, CALIFORNIA

BUILDING SQUARE FOOTAGE:
49,000 SQ. FT.

OWNER:
THE DAVID & LUCILE PACKARD FOUNDATION

ARCHITECT:
EHDD

LANDSCAPE ARCHITECT:
JONI L. JONECKI & ASSOCIATES

SPECIAL THANK YOU TO:

CRAIG NEYMAN, VICE PRESIDENT AND CHIEF FINANCIAL OFFICER, THE DAVID AND LUCILE PACKARD FOUNDATION

BRAD JACOBSON, PROJECT ARCHITECT, EHDD

JONI L. JONECKI, PROJECT LANDSCAPE ARCHITECT, JONI L. JONECKI & ASSOCIATES

CASE STUDY: DAVID & LUCILE PACKARD FOUNDATION | 121

PART II: DESIGN PROCESS

"We took that typical eighty-foot-wide floor plate with private offices on the outside and big workstations on the inside and thought, what if we divide it and pull it apart and create a courtyard in the middle of two forty-foot-wide bays, and then really stretch out this building so there's landscape on the inside and on the outside."

BRAD JACOBSON

The David and Lucile Packard Foundation headquarters is a building that embodies the values that the Foundation supports; one that connects to the context of Los Altos and responds to the California climate. The building takes design inspiration from the "California Living" homes of the 1960s, which emphasized an orientation to the landscape and indoor-outdoor connections. The design team placed an emphasis on beauty and on creating a pleasurable workplace. Comprised of two narrow, forty-foot wide office wings organized around a central courtyard, the design ensures all occupants are within easy reach of daylight, views, and operable windows. Detailed studies were undertaken to test alternatives and optimize the building wings' length, width, and height to ensure a pleasant and welcoming outdoor environment throughout the year. The resulting floorplan layout takes into account both winter warmth and summer cooling and emphasizes spaces that blur the lines between indoors and outdoors.

Staff often choose to take advantage of the inviting California climate and work outside.

CASE STUDY: DAVID & LUCILE PACKARD FOUNDATION | 123

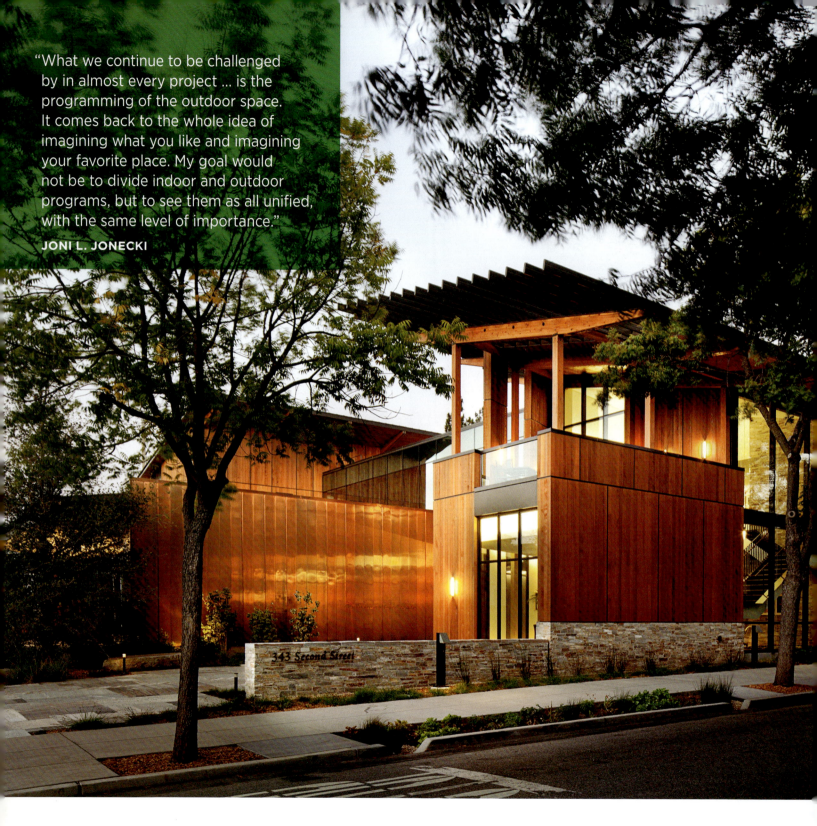

> "What we continue to be challenged by in almost every project ... is the programming of the outdoor space. It comes back to the whole idea of imagining what you like and imagining your favorite place. My goal would not be to divide indoor and outdoor programs, but to see them as all unified, with the same level of importance."
>
> **JONI L. JONECKI**

"In our design workshops, I find it helpful to allow people to daydream of their favorite places....Why do we need to leave it behind? You don't need to go somewhere to experience that healing; that healing can be incorporated into your daily life through simple choices about place and space and making room for nature in your environment."

JONI L. JONECKI

"[One of the goals was] creating a beautiful workplace that suited how people wanted to work and could work most effectively today and in the future, and recognize the changing nature of work and how changing generations like to work."

BRAD JACOBSON

PART III: BUILT EXPERIENCE

With its warm exterior and inviting entry sequence, the building feels more like a home than an office. Staff approach the building along a natural stone walkway, passing by a classic California live oak. Inside, employees work in open "office neighborhoods," but can retreat to small private rooms nearby if they need to. Tall sliding glass doors and operable windows that run all the way down to the floor invite staff to access the views and fresh air.

Just as often, people choose to work in the central courtyard, enjoying the hum of insects in the native meadow grasses or the filtered light under the London plane trees. People in the surrounding neighborhood enjoy the building, too, walking under the preserved shade trees and noticing how the natural materials of the façade—wood, copper, stone, and glass—complement the landscaping.

PART IV: BIOPHILIC ELEMENTS + ATTRIBUTES

LIGHT + SPACE

NATURAL LIGHT: To facilitate daylighting, each of the building wings has a narrow footprint. Light enters through full-height windows and glass doors from both the street and the central courtyard. This ample glazing, in concert with the high ceilings and open floorplans, helps achieve "perceptual brightness"—amply illuminated interiors that require no supplemental artificial light.

FILTERED + DIFFUSED LIGHT: In this sunny climate, light must at times be shaded and filtered to prevent glare and overheating in work spaces. Screens and opaque glass are used to create consistent illumination without distracting shadows and bright spots. The deciduous London plane trees in the courtyard are strategically located to filter sunlight in summer and allow in more light during winter when their branches are bare.

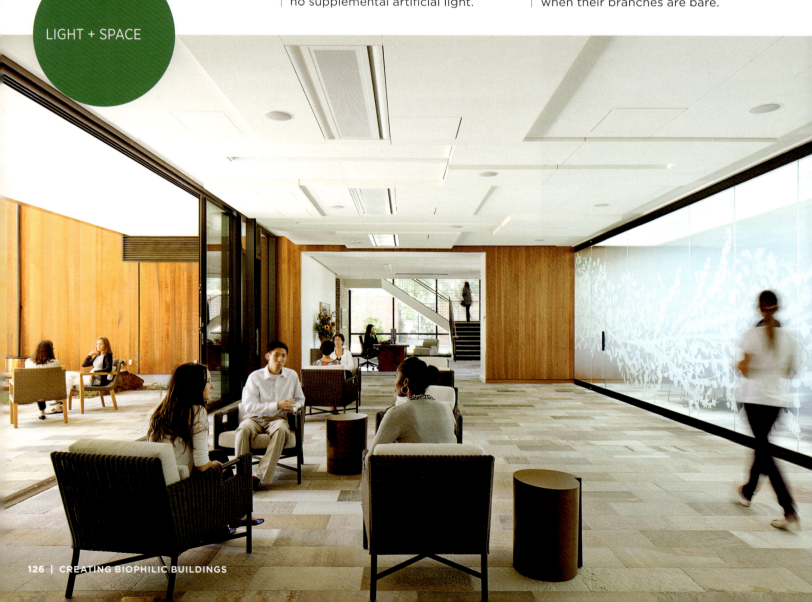

INSIDE-OUTSIDE SPACES: For this project, the outdoor program was just as important as the indoors. Taking advantage of the benign California climate, the design emphasizes the connections between indoor and outdoor spaces, with operable windows and sliding glass doors that invite staff to access the central courtyard. The largest "room" in the project, the courtyard is sheltered on all sides by the building. It functions as a casual meeting space, surrounded by plants native to the California landscape, while other areas, such as the south meadow, provide quiet and serene places for reflection within the public setting. The inside-outside biophilic connection continues even on the second floor, where the boardroom overlooks a green roof planted with a mosaic of succulents.

"You get a sense of materials running indoors to outdoors. The stone is the same in the courtyard and in the entry as it is on the ground floor, so there's this continuity of materials that make you feel like you're connected to the outdoors."

BRAD JACOBSON

"The courtyard really has become a living room. People go out there individually and in pairs all during the day—except maybe in the middle of winter—and really work."

BRAD JACOBSON

Succulents growing on the green roof can be seen from a second-floor board room.

PLACE-BASED RELATIONSHIPS

ECOLOGICAL CONNECTION TO PLACE: The project transformed a site that was mostly impervious to one that supports a productive office while also improving and restoring natural ecological functions. The building achieves net zero energy, captures rainwater, and uses raingardens and swales to treat stormwater, including runoff from an adjacent road. The building design is heavily influenced by the ecology and climate of the central California coast. It is naturally ventilated and illuminated with sunlight, and every occupant enjoys a direct connection to the outside. Mostly native plants in the courtyard create woodland and grassland ecosystems, and the connection to these two ecosystems is reinforced by the themed photographs, etchings, and color palette in each building wing.

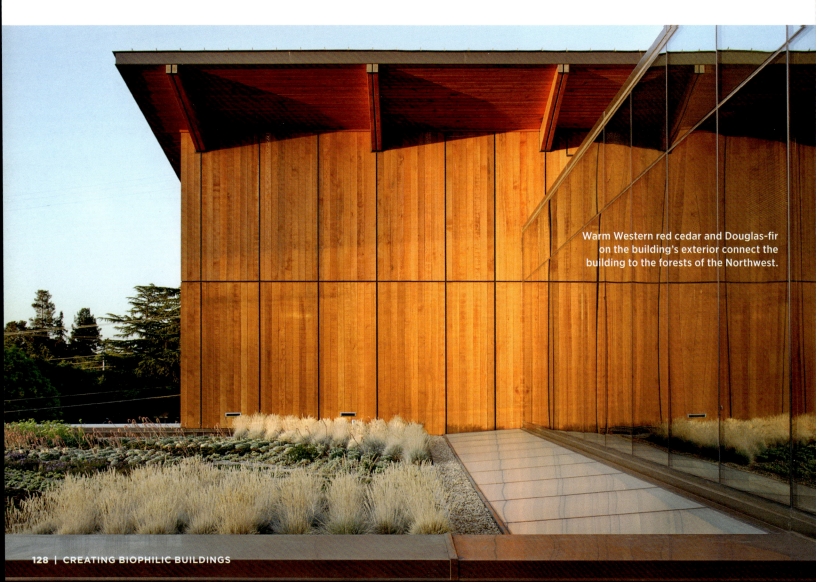

Warm Western red cedar and Douglas-fir on the building's exterior connect the building to the forests of the Northwest.

LANDSCAPE ECOLOGY: More than attractive landscaping, the central courtyard functions as an inviting outdoor room with a variety of seating areas that encourage groups large and small to gather. The central courtyard is planted with native species, and it includes two representative ecosystems—woodland and grassland—divided by a stone drainage channel. By emulating regional ecosystems and habitats, the courtyard connects people to place. The deciduous trees provide shade and cool the building in summer, and the native plants thrive with minimal irrigation or fertilizers and support native flora, including birds, insects, and butterflies.

The landscape was designed to continue through the building and into the surrounding neighborhood. The entry oak, grown from an acorn collected in San Mateo, greets visitors and connects the project to the larger California landscape. Planters along the street protect the existing trees and contribute to the neighborhood feel. A green roof, planted with drought-tolerant succulents, evokes a bluff on the California coastline.

INDIGENOUS MATERIALS: The palette of materials draws from within 500 miles of the project site. The exterior wood siding and overhangs, made from Western red cedar and Douglas-fir from nearby Oregon, provide a richness and color variability that connects occupants to the forests of the region. The interior doors are crafted from salvaged eucalyptus, a tree originally from Australia that has become identified with the California coast. Slate and quartz stones from Mt. Moriah, located on the border of Utah and Nevada, grace the exterior walls and the courtyard walkway, complementing the native plantings and providing continuity throughout the project.

"It was important to bring in a landscape system that is derived from the original plant communities of that region. As people come and go throughout the day, they're walking by the project, going to the courtyards and outdoor spaces. They can touch the plants and the grass seed heads; they can smell the sages, they can see the butterflies, hummingbirds, and the bumblebees—so they are interacting without knowing it, but just fundamentally as part of their daily journey with nature."

JONI L. JONECKI

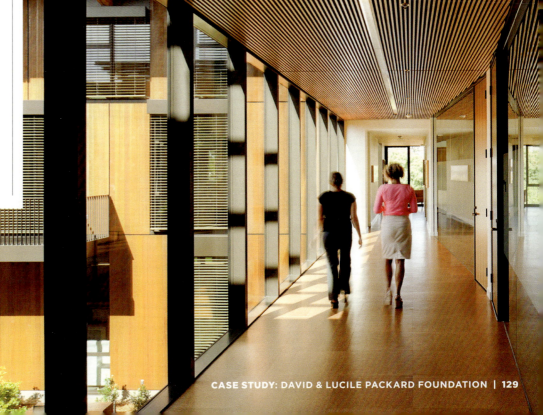

CASE STUDY: DAVID & LUCILE PACKARD FOUNDATION | 129

"As you move around the building, you're always focused in on this courtyard...[The design] brings the landscape through the building in this kind of longitudinal way, so that views are completely uninterrupted through the glass. You can see the landscape across and not only outside of your office window."

BRAD JACOBSON

NATURAL PATTERNS + PROCESSES

CENTRAL FOCAL POINT: The large central courtyard is the heart and soul of the project, and every space opens out to it. On either floor, a person moving around the building is rewarded with a constantly changing view of the courtyard landscape and the building wing beyond. The courtyard is activated by the greenery and the creation of spaces for people to gather, work, and contemplate.

TRANSITIONAL SPACES: The two building wings are connected with "bridges" that house transitional spaces, such as the foyer. These spaces create places to pause and converse when moving from one part of the building to another. Transitional spaces also link the office "neighborhoods" and provide multiple connections with the central courtyard. The "connector spaces" foster collaboration, leaving the office areas for quieter, more focused work.

AGE, CHANGE + THE PATINA OF TIME: While this is a new building, it incorporates materials from the former building, promoting continuity of history and place. The courtyard, particularly the choice of deciduous trees, creates an environment which tracks the changing seasons, with plants that flower and bear seeds and leaves that emerge, change color, and drop. The building exterior, too, will mark the passage of time, as the copper develops a pleasing patina and the Western red cedar siding weathers.

"We did this custom [etching] of an apricot branch on the glass on the movable wall of the large meeting room. This town of Los Altos used to be an apricot orchard. There are still a lot of those trees remaining so that history of the agricultural landscape is remembered."

BRAD JACOBSON

CASE STUDY: DAVID & LUCILE PACKARD FOUNDATION | 131

TE KURA WHARE

PART I:
HEALING FROM WITHIN

PROJECT NAME:
TE KURA WHARE

BUILDING TYPE:
CULTURAL CENTER

LOCATION:
TŪHOE, TĀNEATUA, NEW ZEALAND

BUILDING SQUARE FOOTAGE:
18,800 SQ. FT.

OWNER:
TŪHOE TE URU TAUMATUA

ARCHITECT:
JASMAX

LANDSCAPE ARCHITECT:
TE URU TAUMATUA & JASMAX

SPECIAL THANK YOU TO:

KIRSTI LUKE, CEO, TŪHOE TE URU TAUMATUA

JEROME PARTINGTON, SENIOR ASSOCIATE, JASMAX

Te Kura Whare provides the Tūhoe with a much-needed place where they can gather and celebrate their cultural traditions.

PART II: DESIGN PROCESS

Strategically located at the entrance of the township of Tāneatua, Te Kura Whare serves as a community center and central point of connection for the Ngāi Tūhoe, a Māori *iwi*, or tribe, whose ancestral lands include the steeply forested Te Urewera on New Zealand's North Island. The building provides administration space for the *iwi*, a café, library, and archive of sacred artifacts, as well as a large Tribal Chamber and amphitheater for hosting community events.

Te Kura Whare was created with the intention of restoring pride in the Tūhoe culture and the inherent connection of Tūhoe people to the land, or *mana tangata*. Te Kura Whare was to be much more than a building; it was to be an architectural representation of the Tūhoe people—their beliefs, traditions, culture, and history. The Tūhoe recognized that

the Living Building Challenge could provide a framework to help actualize their intentions. Late architect Ivan Mercep embraced this approach, and his firm, Jasmax and the Tūhoe worked together on the design for several years before the project ever broke ground. This unique collaboration resulted in an exemplary biophilic project that incorporated cultural reverence, spirituality, and a deep respect for nature in every part of the design process.

KO TE WHENUA TE TOTO
O TE TANGATA
The land is the blood of the people
KO TE TANGATA TE
KANOHI O TE WHENUA
The people are the face of the land

TŪHOE PROVERB

"What Tūhoe did that was different and why [Te Kura Whare] is actually different from a lot of Living Buildings is that they did it in a regenerative way. Their purpose was to regenerate their people, to put themselves on the map and to wake themselves up to learn. Everybody in that building can give you a detailed tour of the physics, the build, the materials, where [the materials] came from, and how that building operates and works, from the receptionist up to Kirsti."

JEROME PARTINGTON

The office wing atrium is characterized by dramatic contrasting lighting.

> "The building always reminds me to be open to collaboration…to take on somebody's idea even though you don't understand it. Some of those things you're not going to understand, so the best thing that you can do is trust the person."
>
> **KIRSTI LUKE**

> "We now know about integrative design, about regenerative design—where you're not trying to do a green building but a building that heals the ecosystem and the social system that you're dropping it into. It turns it away from being the object [and] into the relationship."
>
> **JEROME PARTINGTON**

> "What Ivan Mercep had us do in the construction team was respect the design advice that we were bringing, not just as a crazy client, but to show that how our crazy, cultural needs were as relevant as the structural needs of the building—and we achieved it."
>
> **KIRSTI LUKE**

PART III: BUILT EXPERIENCE

Fiercely independent and isolated by rugged, mountainous land, the Tūhoe did not begin feeling the effects of European colonization until the mid-1860s, when the Crown began systematically seizing vital lands from the Tūhoe without their consent. In 2012, the New Zealand government reached a settlement with the Tūhoe, which included financial redress and recognized the Tūhoe as the guardians of their homeland, Te Urewera. Te Kura Whare, which was funded by money received as part of the agreement, presented the Tūhoe people with an opportunity to close the door on the injustices of the past and begin a healing path toward the future. The project also created jobs and provided training for a community with high unemployment and a significant lack of hope.

One of the project's most distinctive features is the powerful wood arch that spans the front of the Tribal Chamber. Tūhoe who enter the building at once feel at home, surrounded by natural wood and natural light. Not only did Tūhoe help design the building, they harvested the timbers, shaped the clay bricks, built the walls, and created the artworks that tell their stories and enhance the building. With pride, they can point out the names etched into the brick walls, teaching their children the importance of connection to place.

Tūhoe enjoy the building in many ways. They attend formal celebrations and ceremonial events in the Tribal Chamber and amphitheater. Outside, people can relax on the building deck or in the shade of the many large trees. Visitors can patronize the Mou Mou Kai Café, where they enjoy *manākitanga*, or hospitality, and connect with members of their community.

PART IV: BIOPHILIC ELEMENTS + ATTRIBUTES

LIGHT + SPACE

LIGHT + SHADOW: Just as the sun streaming through the forest creates pockets of comfort and warmth, this building directs natural light in ways that promote an interplay of light and shadow. Tall, vertical bands of glazing allow light to penetrate the office wing atrium, creating an alternating pattern of light and dark suggestive of tree trunks in a forest. In the café, diagonal stripes of light migrate across the floor, warming the wood and creating bright spots on the stairs. The changing play of light attracts people to different parts of the building at different times of day.

SPATIAL VARIABILITY: Te Kura Whare houses a variety of spaces, from the tribal offices and conference rooms to the café and Tribal Chamber. Each space enjoys a unique scale, spatial quality, and orientation to the sun. The offices are illuminated with a controlled and steady light, reflective of their function, while the café and atrium are distinguished by tall ceilings and dynamic lighting, which changes as the sun moves through the sky. The spacious Tribal Chamber accommodates public ceremonies and celebrations, which are enhanced by the vaulted ceiling, dramatically angled timber posts, and strong and even illumination.

INSIDE-OUTSIDE SPACES: The Tribal Chamber is a dynamic space where people can enjoy shelter from the sun while fresh air sweeps through the open doors. The hall also opens up to a vast outdoor amphitheater. During events, the veranda transforms into a stage, encircled by people sitting or standing on the terraced grass benches. Protected by a large overhang, the generous porch serves as an indoor or outdoor stage, bridging the space between inside and outside.

More than just tribal administration building, Te Kura Whare also includes a library, displays, café and a large Tribal Chamber.

PLACE-BASED RELATIONSHIPS

CULTURAL CONNECTION TO PLACE: Tūhoe identity and culture is inseparable from place and from the land. When their land was taken away, it severed that vital connection and led to decades of disempowerment and despair. With the creation of Te Kura Whare, the Tūhoe sought to begin restoring the relationship between people, culture, and land. Through its architecture and art, through its materials, shaped by Tūhoe hands, through the ceremonies and celebrations that the center hosts and in the archive of cultural artifacts that it houses, Te Kura Whare plays a key role in re-establishing the connection to the land and building pride in Maori culture and traditions.

INTEGRATION OF CULTURE + ECOLOGY: Tu Kura Whare coexists in harmony with the surrounding environment. The project harnesses all of its power from the sun, captures all of its water from the sky and treats all of its waste on site. Tūhoe believe it is their responsibility to nurture,

"Te Kura Whare is an expression of Tūhoe, and because it is of Tūhoe naturally, it is an expression of Te Urewera. Nobody has any right to deny you, your connection, your relationship with that building."

KIRSTI LUKE

"We did not have an expectation that we were building for ourselves a palace; we were trying to sever ourselves from our history of neglect and despair… we came across the idea of the building as a statement of hope and prosperity; hope and optimism."

KIRSTI LUKE

learn from and respect the land. Designing the building to the Living Building Challenge standard helped them create a building endowed with living systems—one that demonstrates the community's values and beliefs.

SPIRIT OF PLACE: The simple materials palette creates a strong connection with the land and identifies the building uniquely within its place. Te Kura Whare is built from wood harvested from forests that are now managed by the Tūhoe people, and the internal walls are composed of 5,000 clay bricks that were created on site as part of a training program for the community. The clay, sourced from various areas of Te Urewera, imparts subtle variations in texture, color and character to the building. The opportunity to fashion earth and wood from their ancestral lands into timber and bricks created memorable experiences which will forever tie the Tūhoe community to the project.

"This building is a living entity and a living representation of the *iwi* ...When you walk into the building you feel its vibrancy, its livingness. It is incredible to walk in there; energetically, it is alive, and it is almost like you can sense the *Mauri* of the building, the spirit of the building."

JEROME PARTINGTON

"The building reminded us of the sophistication of nature, even color clashes in nature—there's no such thing as the business of it. The timber came as it was. If it was in the river, it was darker, dead and down timber depending on the age, and there is something very cool about knowing that a collection of all of those things from nature is specific and unique to us. There's not going to be two shades of that clay or that log, out of that river, out of that gravel. And so that tells you a thing about diversity—it's a beautiful thing."

KIRSTI LUKE

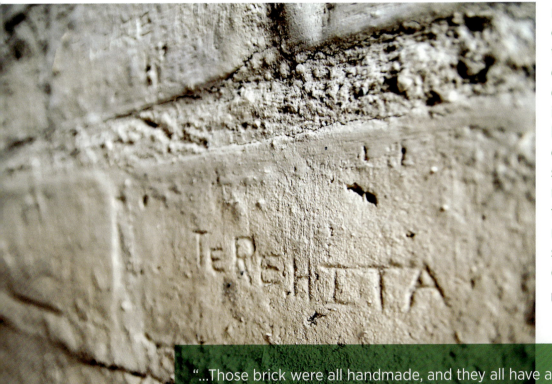

"...Those brick were all handmade, and they all have an identity stamp, be it a name or somebody's handprint. Ivan made one as well. Five thousand personally labeled identified earth bricks, made from clay, and brought to this one building."

JEROME PARTINGTON

NATURAL SHAPES + FORMS

TREE + COLUMNAR SUPPORTS: In Te Kura Whare, natural logs serve as posts, beams, and trusses, emulating the forest and reflecting the vital role trees play in the wellbeing of Tūhoe people. The columnar supports throughout the building are made from pine harvested from Kaingaroa forest, enhancing the cultural connection between the Tūhoe and the forests of the Tūhoe Rohe.

ARCHES, VAULTS + DOMES: The distinctive wooden arch at the entrance to the Tribal Chamber simulates the flight path of *Tama-nui-te-rā* (sun) across the sky, from east to west. The rising of the sun represents potential; with each day comes the opportunity to fulfill dreams and make progress toward goals. In this way the arch encourages Tūhoe to look forward, rather than backward

The imagery on the doors to the Tribal Chamber affirms Tūhoe self determination.

at the bitter legacy of colonialism. Similarly, the vaulted ceiling of the Tribal Chamber is uplifting, enhancing the celebrations held there.

ANIMAL (MOSTLY VERTEBRATE) MOTIFS: The two relief panels that appear beneath the arch at the entrance to the great hall are dedicated to the *whakataukī*, or proverb, *"Tōku Tūhoetanga, Tōku Oranga,"* or *"My Tūhoe Culture, my Prosperity and Salvation."* The unique designs and vivid colors reference and reinforce the notion of *Te Mana Motuhake o Tūhoe*, or self-determination of the Tūhoe people. The *manu*, or bird motif that appears on both panels is inspired by the words of Te Whenuanui: *"Hei hāpai i tēnei manu o te rongomau o te āta noho,"* which means, "To carry on this bird of peace and quietness." The image of the *manu* reminds the viewer of the importance of accessing Tūhoetanga from the past and maintaining it into the present and toward the future. The circular forms symbolize continuation—a way of life introduced at birth and repeated when children grow up and become parents themselves.

The Tūhoe harvested the trees that support the building from forests they themselves manage.

PART I:
EXPRESSING CULTURE

PROJECT NAME:
GLUMAC SHANGHAI OFFICE

BUILDING TYPE:
COMMERCIAL OFFICE

LOCATION:
SHANGHAI, CHINA

BUILDING SQUARE FOOTAGE:
10,000 SQ. FT.

OWNER:
GLUMAC

ARCHITECT:
GENSLER

BIOPHILIC CONSULTANT:
TERRAPIN BRIGHT GREEN

SPECIAL THANK YOU TO:

QUINNIE LI, SUSTAINABILITY MANAGER, GLUMAC SHANGHAI OFFICE

PART II: DESIGN PROCESS

When Glumac had the chance to move their office into the third floor of a 100-year-old mansion in Shanghai's historic Chang Ning District, they jumped at the opportunity. Given the poor outside air quality, creating a healthy indoor environment was paramount. Taking guidance from Terrapin Green's 14 Patterns of Biophilic Design, which coalesce Kellert's Elements and Attributes into simple categories, the team focused on creating visual connections to nature, incorporating natural shapes and forms, bringing dynamic and diffused lighting into the space and promoting healthy indoor air. Combining these biophilic elements with traditional Chinese motifs and materials that recognize the building's historic context, the transformed office celebrates the heritage of its site and ensures the health and comfort of its occupants.

"From an operator perspective, it's so much easier to hire people by bringing them into this office. It's easier for us to attract the right talent because the office is so comfortable and so bright."

QUINNIE LI

The design team focused on creating comfortable spaces enhanced with natural light and natural shapes and forms.

PART III: BUILT EXPERIENCE

"Do not focus on one element alone and just go down that path because you love it so much. It has to be an integrative solution. Don't just do one thing because it's beautiful; it also has to be functional, operations friendly and user friendly."

QUINNIE LI

"For Glumac Shanghai, biophilic design provides a comfortable bridge to teaching sustainable design because the benefits are personal and speak to employee satisfaction, health and wellbeing. These are health outcomes that are important everywhere, but especially critical in places like Shanghai where people feel the health impacts from a degraded environment on a daily basis."

FROM BIOPHILIC DESIGN NARRATIVE

As you approach Glumac's office you are welcomed by the "lucky clouds" stenciled on the entry doors; immediately upon entering, you are struck by the three-dimensional cloud structures that wind through the space, inviting exploration. Natural daylight fills the open offices and bistro, and the ample windows and wide terrace provide views to the lush courtyard below. Many take advantage of this sheltered sunny space for napping after lunch. The plants growing on the green wall and in pots throughout the office complement the cloud structures, creating a biophilic environment that connects occupants with nature even while protecting them from poor air quality outdoors.

The "cloud sculptures" mitigate noise but also introduce a flowing and whimsical organic element into the office.

PART IV: BIOPHILIC ELEMENTS + ATTRIBUTES

ENVIRONMENTAL FEATURES

COLOR: In bright hues that evoke apples, lime, grass, and new leaves, the color green is used to infuse freshness and a visual cohesiveness to the office space. In the carpet and chair cushions, in the tile backsplash in the bistro kitchen and the translucent partition, and even in the computer screen savers, green accents connect with the Kvatrat cloud installation and the live plants to create a coherent and calming space.

VIEWS + VISTAS: Every desk in the space has a view to the outside, and the conference room and collaborative work areas incorporate floor-to-ceiling windows and glass doors

The color green provides continuity throughout the spaces.

150 | CREATING BIOPHILIC BUILDINGS

which open up to the terrace. There, occupants can enjoy views of the leafy canopy of mature trees and the lush understory of plants in the garden courtyard below, the historic buildings nearby, and the skyscrapers in the distance.

PLANTS: Glumac employees enjoy intimate contact with nature through the plants on the green wall and the potted plants scattered throughout the office. The plants bring color into the space and connect with the garden courtyard, but they also contribute to good indoor air quality—an important consideration for occupants, as the building is located in a district known for its polluted air. The living wall is dominated by *Sansevieria trifasciata*, or mother-in-law's tongue, which was chosen for its air-filtering qualities.

"When you look out, you see history."

QUINNIE LI

A wall of pollutant-filtering plants improves air quality in the office.

CASE STUDY: GLUMAC SHANGHAI OFFICE | 151

NATURAL SHAPES + FORMS

SHAPES RESISTING STRAIGHT LINES + RIGHT ANGLES: One of the most striking features in the renovated office is the Kvadrat cloud installations that are incorporated throughout the space. Designed by internationally acclaimed designers Ronan and Erwan Bouroullec in collaboration with Danish firm Kvatrat, the "clouds" are made from triangular textile panels arranged in three-dimensional pyramids. The pyramids can then be stitched together to create an endless variety of organic shapes. Inspired by cultural symbols such as dragons and clouds, Glumac employees pieced the clouds together themselves, creating a pleasing pattern of green, white, gray, and black shapes that curve around ceilings, walls, and columns. Not only do these installations provide a playful and softening balance to an otherwise rectilinear space, they also provide an important sound-absorbing function.

SIMULATION OF NATURAL FEATURES: The Chinese consider clouds auspicious, and cloud motifs appear frequently in Chinese art and architecture. In the Glumac office, Chinese "lucky clouds" are incorporated into the glass entry doors as graceful swirls, which are echoed in the intricately engraved stools across from the reception desk. The naturalistic pattern in the carpeting is suggestive of wispy cirrus clouds or flowing water.

BIOMORPHY: A "dragon" wraps around a column in the bistro. Clouds float across the wall behind the reception desk. Excellent examples of biomorphy, the Kvadrat clouds use simple geometry to create complex and surprising structures that suggest natural phenomena and living organisms. Along with the other biophilic features, these symbolic elements help create a unique and stimulating office environment for Glumac Shanghai's employees.

> "Everything in this office cannot just be beautiful because that doesn't pass our budget sheet; it has to have a function. The art piece has a really good acoustic value, better than carpets."
>
> **QUINNIE LI**

The Kvadrat "cloud" sculptures suggest the forms of animals and other natural phenomena.

SUSTAINABLE BUILDINGS RESEARCH CENTRE

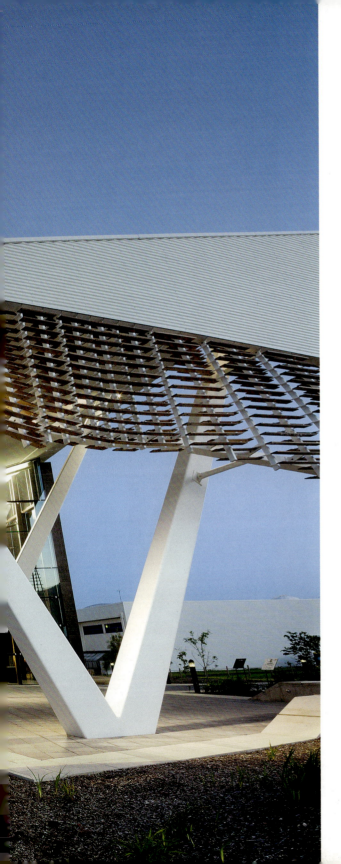

PART I: PRACTICING BIOPHILIC DESIGN

PROJECT NAME:
SUSTAINABLE BUILDINGS RESEARCH CENTRE (SBRC)

BUILDING TYPE:
UNIVERSITY RESEARCH FACILITY

LOCATION:
WOLLONGONG, AUSTRALIA

BUILDING SQUARE FOOTAGE:
31,355 SQ. FT.

OWNER:
UNIVERSITY OF WOLLONGONG AUSTRALIA

ARCHITECT:
COX ARCHITECTURE

LANDSCAPE ARCHITECT:
TAYLOR BRAMMER

SPECIAL THANK YOU TO:

PAUL COOPER, DIRECTOR, SUSTAINABLE BUILDINGS RESEARCH CENTRE

MICHAEL BRADBURN, PROJECT ARCHITECT, COX ARCHITECTURE

CASE STUDY: SUSTAINABLE BUILDINGS RESEARCH CENTRE | 155

PART II: DESIGN PROCESS

The Sustainable Buildings Research Centre (SBRC), part of the University of Wollongong's Innovation Campus, was created to test and demonstrate technologies that will inspire the green building movement in Australia. Wollongong is a few hours south of Sydney, on the beautiful New South Wales coast, and the Centre is situated between a mountain and the sea.

Composed of two buildings linked by a landscaped courtyard and bridge, the Centre demonstrates the practices and research it supports and responds to the climate and coastal breezes. In materiality and design, the Centre reflects the beauty and resiliency of the Australian coastal landscape and connects occupants with nature, no matter where they are in the buildings.

"We work in this environment where people can just make their lunches here, use food from the garden, and walk outside; it doesn't matter what the weather is because we've got spaces that are attuned to different times of the year, rain or shine. Although I'm an engineer and play with numbers all the time, to me, you can't measure the value of that through any quantitative metric scale."

PAUL COOPER

"Prior to adopting the Living Building Challenge, Paul had come to us and started showing us things that he wanted to be referenced within the building. He brought us photos of bluebottles, driftwood, and of the beach—things that were very much of the place. We used those items as inspiration for some of the finer details in the building where we brought in natural patterns and processes."

MICHAEL BRADBURN

CASE STUDY: SUSTAINABLE BUILDINGS RESEARCH CENTRE | 157

A landscaped corridor and bridge connect the two wings of the SBRC.

PART III: BUILT EXPERIENCE

The Centre's two buildings—one housing administration and programs, and another containing hands-on research labs—are connected by an open deck and landscaped corridor. As the happy "guinea pigs" who enjoy the benefits of a building designed to engage occupants with the natural environment, students and researchers conduct hands-on research in bright, open spaces that encourage collaboration. They prepare lunch in the centrally located kitchen and enjoy eating outside among the native plants. Students and researchers can choose from sheltered outdoor work spaces or indoor workstations, where through the open windows, they can enjoy the sound of birds chattering and smell the hint of ocean spray riding in on the wind. Visitors can take in a performance in the outdoor exhibition space or learn about the Centre's projects in the open exhibition room, where inspiring views of the Illawara escarpment can be glimpsed through double-height windows.

PART IV: BIOPHILIC ELEMENTS + ATTRIBUTES

LIGHT + SPACE

LIGHT + SHADOW: In response to the harsh Australian sun, the building carefully controls light with shading and overhangs while still providing abundant daylighting in all of the working spaces. Daylight in the transitional and public areas is brighter and vivid, with contrasting shadows that enliven the spaces. The dramatic shade structure with its biomorphic curve protects the building's west side while casting complex shadows into the spaces below.

INSIDE-OUTSIDE SPACES: The building is integrated into the landscape, with outdoor courtyards that blur the lines between inside and outside. Splitting the campus into two buildings, with plantings

Large, light-filled volumes create a sense of spaciousness.

"The lighting in the exhibition space changes by the hour." **PAUL COOPER**

and wetlands in between, naturally encourages people to engage with the landscaping. Large open decks between the buildings provide places to gather and dwell, while floor-to-ceiling walls of glass connect the interior public spaces to the outside. The atrium, with its green walls and high ceiling, creates a light-filled space that feels like it is as much outdoors as indoors, and sheltered benches along an outside wall provide places to work that are protected from the sun.

SPACIOUSNESS: The building form creates light-filled spaces that relate to the outside and respond to climate. Upon entering, occupants and visitors encounter the lofty exhibition space, distinguished by its double-height glass walls. Elsewhere, the sloping roof, two-story green wall and central staircase create a sense of spaciousness that reflects the open and transparent spirit of collaboration the Centre was designed to cultivate.

The dramatic overhang highlights the equally dramatic Illawarra escarpment in the background.

PLACE-BASED RELATIONSHIPS

"[Even with] our energy systems, from the very beginning we always talked about the building being more akin to an organism."

PAUL COOPER

ECOLOGICAL CONNECTION TO PLACE: With climate modulated by the Pacific Ocean, the region enjoys warm summers that hover in the mid-80s and mild winters with temperatures that rarely drop below 50 degrees. The building form responds to climate and ecology with a dramatic roof structure that reaches out to the Illawarra escarpment to the west; generous overhangs elsewhere prevent the spaces from overheating and minimize energy use. Large operable windows provide occupants with fresh air and views of the native coastal plants in the courtyard. From almost anywhere in the building, people can witness the daily and seasonal variations in weather, changing quality of light, and the passing of clouds.

LANDSCAPE ECOLOGY: Native landscaping, including a wetland corridor, integrates the building with the site and extends beyond it to the

162 | CREATING BIOPHILIC BUILDINGS

"Wherever we used reclaimed timber, we wanted to not hide that, so if you look at the detail within the joinery or the columns that hold up the main roof structure over the office, they all tell a story of where they come from. You can see one edge has been left in the state that it was found, and the various holes from its previous life."

MICHAEL BRADBURN

greater campus. Plantings adapted to the coastal environment soften the building edges, allowing the Centre to merge and mature with the landscape. A garden dominated by bush tucker, a bush species valued by indigenous people for food and medicine, connects staff, students and visitors to the indigenous cultural heritage and instructs occupants on how landscaping can provide food as well as beauty. Sheltered spaces around and between the building provide opportunities to rest and appreciate the wider landscape, including the escarpment views to the west, Puckeys Estate to the east, and the more intimate environs of the bush tucker garden.

SPIRIT OF PLACE: The Centre is oriented between the Pacific Ocean and the striking Illawarra escarpment. The grand steel canopy at the building entrance, inspired by vernacular Australian sheds, protects visitors from the sun while framing and echoing this distinctive landmark. Steel supports saved from old rail lines, weathered timber recycled from old bridges, and reclaimed bricks salvaged from some of Sydney's buildings ground the Centre in its particular place and tie it in with stories from Australia's past. The landscape plantings and hardscape materials complement the building, creating a project that is at once harsh and beautiful, much like the Australian landscape itself.

NATURAL PATTERNS + PROCESSES

The variety of earth tones, textures and shapes create a visually stimulating exterior.

SENSORY VARIABILITY: The design deliberately creates journeys through space which engage all the senses and invite students, staff, and visitors to explore and experience the Centre. Framed views and vistas inspire occupants in both public and private spaces, and the varied textures and patterns in the building materials and landscape plants encourage people not just to look, but to touch and feel. Occupants are encouraged to harvest and taste the fruits and vegetables from the garden, including the native bush plants. The courtyard is filled with birdsong and the sound of wind rushing through the leaves of the landscape plants. During summer and spring, building interiors fill with the fragrance of fresh air coming from the mountains, the tang of coastal dune plants, and the scent of citrus blossoms.

TRANSITIONAL SPACES: The deliberate decision to divide the programming between two buildings, with landscaped areas in between, ensures that occupants will spend at least part of their day outside on their way from one building to the other. These pedestrian journeys foster direct connections with nature, and the variety of pathways and spaces spark creativity, teaching, and learning.

COMPLEMENTARY CONTRASTS: The contrast of materials and their functionality are celebrated throughout the building. The substantial V-shaped supports contrast with the almost delicate tapestry of wood members that cascade from the steel roof canopy. A balustrade detail in the entrance lobby, composed of wood and laminated glass which lets light pass through, resembles the texture of a bluebottle, a small blue jellyfish which is both beautiful and yet dangerous. Reused and reclaimed lumber, used extensively throughout the project, was left in its found state and celebrated in exposed installations, revealing the natural processes of weathering and staining. Variegated bricks; horizontal and vertical wood siding and shade structures; the ribbing on the underside of the metal overhangs—all of these contrasting textures and colors come together to create visually stimulating façades that complement the native landscape. Similarly, the blooms of color that ebb and flow throughout the year mark the seasons and contrast beautifully with the timber and unfinished brickwork.

BULLITT CENTER

PART I:
A TREE IN THE CITY

PROJECT NAME:
BULLITT CENTER

BUILDING TYPE:
COMMERCIAL OFFICE

LOCATION:
SEATTLE, WASHINGTON

BUILDING SQUARE FOOTAGE:
52,000 SQ. FT.

OWNER:
BULLITT FOUNDATION

ARCHITECT:
MILLER HULL

LANDSCAPE ARCHITECT:
BERGER PARTNERSHIP

SPECIAL THANK YOU TO:

DENIS HAYES, PRESIDENT AND CEO, BULLITT FOUNDATION

BRIAN COURT, PRINCIPAL ARCHITECT, MILLER HULL

MARGARET SPRUG, DESIGN PARTNER, MILLER HULL

JONATHAN MORLEY, LANDSCAPE ARCHITECT, BERGER PARTNERSHIP

PART II: DESIGN PROCESS

Located in a dense urban neighborhood near downtown Seattle, the six-story Bullitt Center was the first commercial office building to be fully certified as a Living Building. The design team set out to create a building that would last at least 250 years—a lifespan closer to that of a tree than of today's typical buildings. The trees of the Pacific Northwest served as the building's inspiration and its central metaphor. The building form consists of exposed structural wood beams and ceilings and a "canopy" of solar modules that still allow in plenty of light through the skylights. With health and wellness of occupants at the forefront, the team designed the building to provide all occupants with access to daylight and fresh air. An "irresistible staircase" serves as the main means of moving through the building, connecting tenants with views of the city and each other.

The site was surrounded by three streets, one a busy thoroughfare linking downtown Seattle to Lake Washington. As part of the project development, one of these streets was permanently closed, creating a pedestrian plaza between the building and a neighborhood pocket park called McGlivra Park. By cultivating an ecosystem of integrated indoor and outdoor spaces, the building has brought the block to life.

> "We wanted to have a building that functioned like an organism."
> **DENIS HAYES**

> "With the Bullitt Center, a lot of the practices or design strategies were about relearning stuff that we've been taught to forget as architects. With cheap energy, we started designing buildings that didn't have the potential to operate passively. But these old warehouse buildings designed at the turn of the century had all of these lessons baked in—higher floors; bigger windows; natural materials."
>
> BRIAN COURT

PART III: BUILT EXPERIENCE

Anyone who visits the Bullitt Center for the first time is struck by the distinctive solar canopy and the beauty of the wood structure. Visitors and tenants alike are drawn to the "irresistible" staircase, where they can enjoy the evolving views of the city and the changing patterns of light and shadow. In the open office environment, tenants continue to enjoy the access to views and fresh air through the floor-to-ceiling windows. The grove of 100-year-old plane trees that grace McGilvra Park are a constant presence, both inside and outside the building. Building tenants—and on occasion, students and passersby—can be seen playing ping-pong in the park or sitting in the sun on the plaza's wood benches.

"We had to set aside our typical processes and look at it with fresh eyes; we had to trust in the process. This gets to the spirit of the Living Building Challenge and biophilic design—trying to solve problems the way nature would solve them. You're not bringing intellectual baggage to it; [instead], you're letting systems drive the form and you're making each system as efficient as possible. Let the building design itself, as if it were evolving as an organism."

BRIAN COURT

"Trees as living things are the inspiration for what this building is and does: producing their own power, mitigating storm water, generating the energy that you need to be self-sustaining."

JONATHAN MORLEY

CASE STUDY: BULLITT CENTER | 171

PART IV: BIOPHILIC ELEMENTS + ATTRIBUTES

ENVIRONMENTAL FEATURES

AIR: The Bullitt Center relies on natural ventilation, with fully operable windows that allow the building to breathe in response to the weather. When the windows are open, breezes circulate through the spaces, connecting the occupants to the sounds and smells of the surrounding urban neighborhood. Serving as a transition space linking inside and outside, the irresistible staircase is not heated. Instead, it is ventilated with fresh air and maintains the same temperature as outside, providing those who choose the stairs over the tucked-away elevator with a multisensory experience, along with some physical activity.

NATURAL MATERIALS: The Bullitt Center is the first timber-framed structure to be permitted in Seattle since the 1920s. The exposed glulam structural members and wood ceilings, sourced from regional and FSC-certified forests, connect the occupants of the building to the

> "We hear from people—and I notice it when I'm there—that the stairwell smells really fresh, [resulting from] the combination of the wood and the open windows and it just being an unconditioned space."
>
> **MARGARET SPRUG**

> "As you walk through any of our floors, you find yourself surrounded by something that, while not a natural forest, is an approximation of it, by bringing something that is alive and botanical and part of the kind of environment we evolved with. It grounds you a little bit, I think."
>
> **DENIS HAYES**

> "A primary strategy incorporated into the building's design was to move the main exit stair out beyond the face of the building and create an 'irresistible stair' for human delight—a transparent glass stairwell located on an outside wall, which among other health and social benefits, offers dramatic views of the city skyline, Puget Sound, and the Olympic Mountains— to connect people with their exquisite surroundings."
>
> **BRIAN COURT**

great conifer forests of the Pacific Northwest, and the natural wood palette brings warmth and texture to this urban environment.

VIEWS + VISTAS: The building's long vertical windows create a strong connection to the outdoor environment, from street to sky. Most floors provide distant glimpses of Mount Rainier as well as close views of the trunks and leafy branches of the plane trees in nearby McGilvra Park.

From within the building, people can enjoy a unique perspective, looking down on the green canopy of the urban forest with the geometry of high-rise buildings in the distance. The irresistible staircase frames views of downtown Seattle and the Puget Sound, connecting the building to the city and its region and compelling people up the flights to the final landing, where they are rewarded with expansive views framed by the overhanging solar canopy.

LIGHT + SPACE

NATURAL LIGHT: In a region prone to overcast winter days and rain, it was especially important to welcome as much natural light into the building as possible. On each floor, tall ceilings with large, full-height vertical windows allow light to penetrate deeply into the building, filling the spaces with bright and dynamically changing light. Workstations are open, allowing the light to proliferate throughout the offices. Natural light also fills the staircase, highlighting the warm wood tones of the stair treads. Throughout the building, the combination of natural light on wood grain connects people with the natural environment, right in the heart of the city.

SPACIOUSNESS: Occupants experience spaciousness on different scales, depending on where they are in the building. With its soaring ceiling, the lobby is an airy volume grounded by cement columns.

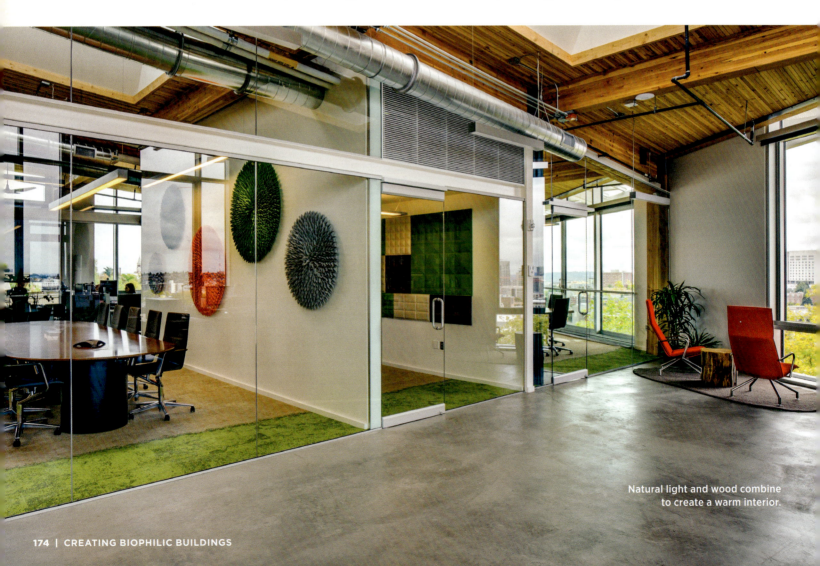

Natural light and wood combine to create a warm interior.

In the office environment, generous floor-to-ceiling heights and open layouts contribute to the feeling of spaciousness. Full-height windows invite light to bounce through the spaces; these vertical bands of glass extend to the ceilings, which seem to float above them. The staircase, composed of wood, steel, and transparent glass, functions as an outdoor room in an indoor space.

LIGHT + SHADOW: When the sun shines, stripes of sun and shadow move across the floor of the Bullitt Center, marking time and season and orienting people to place. When animated with light, the staircase becomes a functional sculpture. The stair treads filter incoming sunlight, casting diagonally patterned shadows on the walls and on the flights and floors below. As clouds gather and disperse, occupants experience the gradations of light and connect with outside conditions.

> "We wanted it to be warm and enriching. That was about the wood structure and windows and getting the natural light onto the wood structure. We were constantly trying to make sure that [these two elements] were always working together."
>
> **BRIAN COURT**

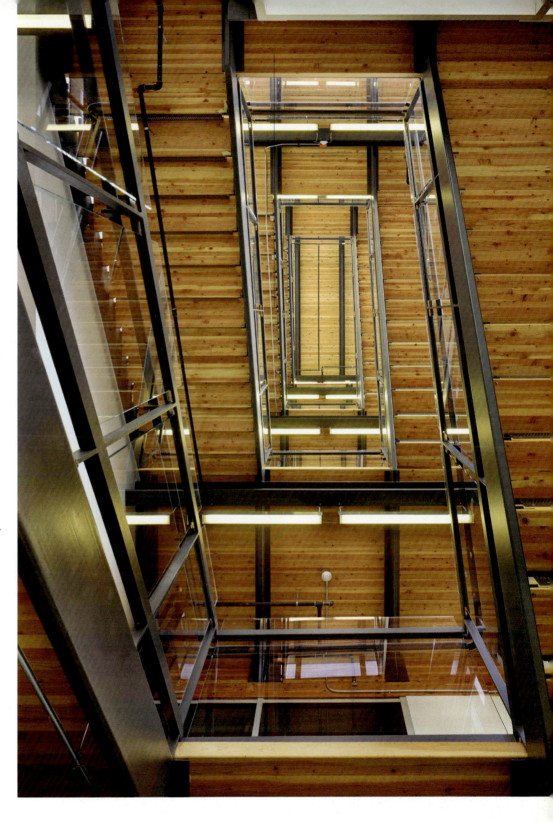

GOOGLE CHICAGO

PART I: CONNECTING TO HISTORICAL CONTEXT

PROJECT NAME:
GOOGLE CHICAGO

BUILDING TYPE:
COMMERCIAL OFFICE

LOCATION:
CHICAGO, ILLINOIS

BUILDING SQUARE FOOTAGE:
237,198 SQ. FT.

OWNER:
GOOGLE

ARCHITECT:
VOA

SUSTAINABILITY CONSULTANT:
CBRE

....

SPECIAL THANK YOU TO:

PRIYA PREMCHANDRAN, [E]TEAM DESIGN AND CONSTRUCTION LEAD, GOOGLE REAL ESTATE WORKPLACE AND SERVICES (REWS)

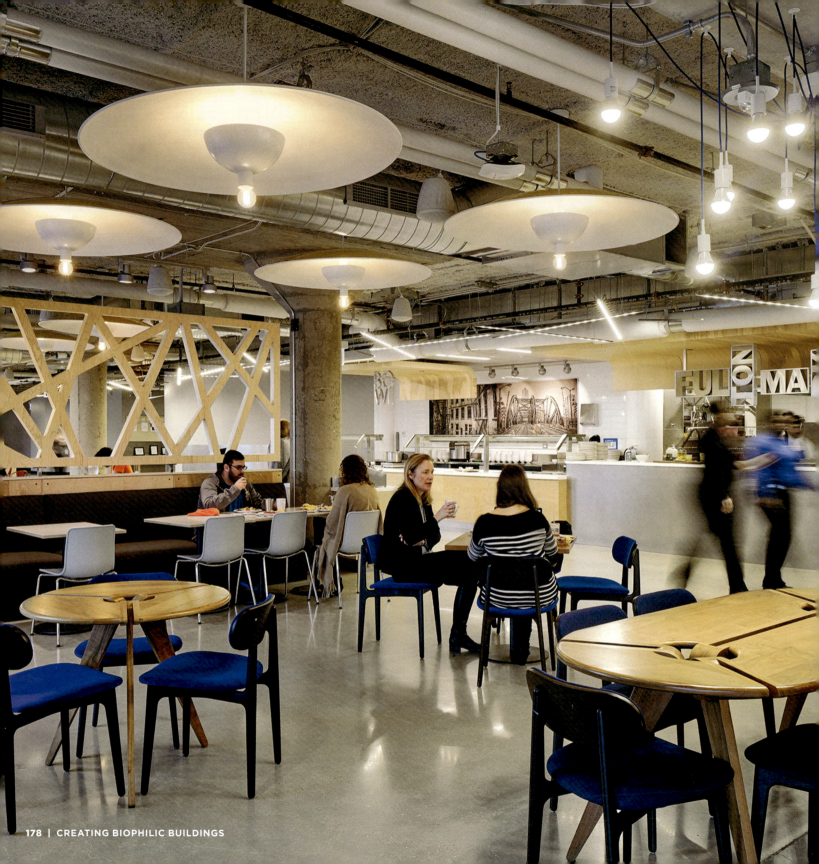

PART II: DESIGN PROCESS

Google Chicago Headquarters is located in the city's historic West Loop neighborhood. The seven-floor office was formerly a windowless cold storage warehousing facility. The transformed space includes a dedicated lobby for Google employees, conference space, themed office, meeting space, and a café with a full-service kitchen.

The design team focused on creating healthy environments that inspire and empower employees. Early on, Google held a visioning session with the future building occupants and compiled wish lists and ideas. A small group of employees worked with the design team throughout the process to provide feedback on features that would directly affect the employees' work environment. The final design preserves the industrial bones of the historic building while facilitating effective daylighting and strong connections with the outdoors while creating central gathering places where employees can come together.

Unique art installations celebrate Chicago history on every floor.

PART III: BUILT EXPERIENCE

By transforming a windowless cold storage warehousing facility into a vibrant, light-filled space, Google Chicago's new office exemplifies neighborhood revitalization. The design provides naturally lit spaces with direct visual connections to the outdoors and establishes connections to both the building and to Chicago's rich neighborhood history. In the open offices and conference rooms, occupants appreciate inspiring views of the Chicago skyline, and as they take advantage of amenities such as the game room and café, they enjoy the Chicago-themed installations that distinguish each floor. Most eschew the elevator in favor of the "conversational stair," where employees meet and linger on the generous landings, enjoying the natural light that filters through the atrium from above.

"Without the design elements that we have incorporated into the project, the project would not represent the location and function intended. In other words, it would be a office that could be located anywhere in the world and it would not have the impact on its occupants as desired initially."

PRIYA PREMCHANDRAN

"Biophilic design needs to be integrated into the overall design process and should include all members of the team, including end users. Biophilic design can be used as a strong framework informing and influencing design such that the outcomes feel part of the overall project rather than added on."

PRIYA PREMCHANDRAN

"Biophilic Design drove the design to be more focused on the spirit of the place and to connect people with the place. This focus was important as it created a common purpose and a unifying language for all the design decisions made on the project and put user experience in the center of those decisions."

PRIYA PREMCHANDRAN

Large windows bring in natural light and inspiring views of the city.

LIGHT + SPACE

PART IV: BIOPHILIC ELEMENTS + ATTRIBUTES

NATURAL LIGHT: One of the project goals was to carefully create daylit spaces that would promote the body's natural circadian rhythms, which can improve productivity and reduce low-level stress. Occupants access natural light through the open offices along the perimeter of the building and through the multistory atrium. In the more interior spaces, occupants can adjust the color temperature of their task lights, ensuring that they benefit from a full spectrum of light no matter where they are in the building.

SPATIAL VARIABILITY: The process of transforming these seven floors into a healthy, biophilic workplace created spaces that vary in scale and function. Glass-lined conference rooms provide inspiring views of the cityscape and into other conference rooms. A latticework partition creates cozy seating areas in the café without blocking views. From the six-story atrium to the light-filled café, with its dramatic views of the city, these spaces stimulate and rejuvenate employees and provide ample opportunities for them to interact with each other and connect with the outdoor views.

SPACIOUSNESS: The large atrium serves as the central "piazza" for Google Chicago's employees. This volume casts sunlight down onto each floor and creates a sense of spaciousness which instinctively attracts everyone in the building. The more sheltered spaces adjacent to the staircase and atrium take advantage of the natural light and visual connections to floors above and below, while in the open office areas, full-height windows seem to extend the workspaces past the walls and into the cityscape beyond.

"Google wanted to provide the occupants with a direct connection to the outside. The large atrium provides the connectivity between people of different floors as well as a connection to the outside throughout the day. The temporal connection to the natural environment is also achieved with a direct view to the outside from each seated workspace. The carefully designed roof space is designed to be functional during all seasons including winter."

PRIYA PREMCHANDRAN

CASE STUDY: GOOGLE CHICAGO | 183

PLACE-BASED RELATIONSHIPS

HISTORICAL CONNECTION TO PLACE: 1000 West Fulton Market was built in 1923 as a state-of-the-art cold storage warehouse. The original building was stark and windowless. Instead of covering up the original industrial structure, the design team chose to celebrate it, complementing and softening the strong concrete elements with warmer materials, natural light, rounded light fixtures and furniture, live plants, art, and curving walls. Through this approach, the design team was able to create a healthy and productive work environment while celebrating the building's history and context. These historic architectural elements provide continuity with the past, even though the function of these floors is very different from their original purpose.

The renovation preserved and highlighted the structure of the historic building.

CULTURAL CONNECTION TO PLACE: The project team skillfully manipulated the attributes of light and space to create a central piazza that functions as a community center and encourages Google employees to interact and socialize. The design creates other unique spaces throughout the building, including micro-kitchens, a game room, music studio, and maker space, which connect people with each other and that support the distinct culture of Google.

AVOIDING PLACELESSNESS: Embracing Chicago's rich neighborhoods and architectural history, each of the seven office floors is distinguished by a theme that celebrates a different aspect of the city, from its famous parks to its iconic transit systems. Art installations draw from historical references. Transposed on the exposed industrial structure, these elements helps create a project that seems distinctly of its place while also meeting all of the company's modern programming needs and fostering a healthy and productive work environment.

Bold graphics and bright colors contribute to the sensory variability in the Google Chicago offices.

NATURAL PATTERNS + PROCESSES

SENSORY VARIABILITY: The dynamic video walls; edible plants; varying textures and shapes in the finishes and fixtures—on every floor and in every space, there is something to simulate and provoke curiosity. Bold and vibrant art and graphics give each level a unique identity and vividly portray aspects of Chicago's identity and past. The undulating walls and diversity of work spaces and seating arrangements, which include brightly colored biomorphic furniture, enliven the office, while graphic signage informs occupants and visitors about the sustainable features of the building. The sensory variability encourages creative collaboration and original thought.

BOUNDED SPACES: The design creates places of refuge throughout the project—places with discrete functions, where employees can feel protected but not cut off. These places include elements which clearly mark boundaries while not blocking access or views. Seating areas in the café are protected with lower ceilings and a latticework partition. Similarly, seating areas adjacent to the stairwell and expansive atrium are protected by lower ceilings and aluminum railings but still enjoy access to the views and natural light.

INTEGRATION OF PARTS TO WHOLE: While the themed installations and historical art pieces mark each area of the Google office with a unique identity, the atrium serves as a central focal point and brings all of these diverse elements into a cohesive whole. Together with the staircase, the atrium orients people no matter where they are in the building and provides physical and visual connections to each floor. Similarly, the concrete columns and ceilings provide cohesiveness from floor to floor and space to space, even as other elements change. The views of the city and the repetition of certain elements, such as the undulating walls, also serve as a unifying elements, reminding occupants that they are all working toward common goals.

"To be human is to become visible
while carrying what is hidden as a gift to others.
To remember the other world in this world
is to live in your true inheritance.

You are not a troubled guest on this earth,
you are not an accident amidst other accidents
you were invited from another and greater night
than the one from which you have just emerged.

Now, looking through the slanting
light of the morning window
toward the mountain presence of
everything that can be…"

DAVID WHYTE

CREATING HABITAT FOR HUMANS:
TOOLS & RESOURCES

The fourteen projects highlighted in this book are diverse in type, size, location, and climate, but consistent in creating habitat for humans and connecting people and nature. The projects that were the most successful at implementing biophilic design are the ones that connect most deeply to their place. The design teams that took extensive time to understand the ecology and culture of the site and region created buildings that express an extra dimension of spirit and tranquility and dissolve the separation between the inside and the outside. For example, the Josey Pavilion's connection to the North Texas Prairie is so strong that the building itself becomes a translator between people and nature, rather than simply a shelter from the elements. Te Kura Whare is much more than a building that houses social service programs; it provides a place in the heart of the Tūhoe homeland where the rich Tūhoe culture can once more thrive and be celebrated. Both of these projects share distinct relationships with the land, the people and their histories and could not be built in any other place.

Multisensory design is another consistent theme that emerged in the more dynamic projects. Spaces that engage hearing, smell, and touch, in addition to the visual sense help occupants to feel connected to their community, place, and each

Bullitt Center

KELLERT'S BIOPHILIC DESIGN ELEMENTS & ATTRIBUTES: CASE STUDY USE

ENVIRONMENTAL FEATURES

- Color ●
- Water ●
- Air ● ●
- Natural ventilation
- Plants ● ● ●
- Animals
- Natural materials ● ●
- Views and vistas ● ● ● ●
- Façade greening
- Geology and landscape ●
- Habitats and ecosystems ●
- Fire

NATURAL SHAPES + FORMS

- Botanical motifs ●
- Tree and columnar supports ●
- Animal (mainly vertebrate) motifs ●
- Shells and spirals
- Egg, oval and tubular forms
- Arches, vaults, domes ●
- Shapes resisting straight lines and right angles ● ●
- Simulation of natural features ● ●
- Biomorphy ●
- Geomorphology
- Biomimicry ●

NATURAL PATTERNS + PROCESSES

- Sensory variability ● ● ● ●
- Information richness ● ● ●
- Age, change and the patina of time ●
- Growth and efflorescence
- Central focal point ● ● ● ● ●
- Patterned wholes
- Bounded spaces ●
- Transitional spaces ● ● ●
- Linked series and chains ●
- Integration of parts to wholes ●
- Complementary contrasts ●
- Dynamic balance and tension
- Fractals ●
- Hierarchically organized ratios and scales

---

other. At the Phipps Center for Sustainable Landscapes, evocative sounds from the region enliven the atrium and invite people to pause and interact. At the R.W. Kern Center, the interactive puzzles create an atmosphere of play and community as people explore solutions.

Spaces created specifically for people to gather and interact as a community—the magnificent atrium at the Mosaic Centre and the irresistible stairs at the Bullitt Center, for example—foster a stronger connection to place. These projects show that biophilic design does not show up only in one way; rather, it is multifaceted, promoting repeated and variable experiences that allow people to connect with nature on many levels and in many ways.

WHAT CAN WE LEARN FROM THE CASE STUDIES?
Assessing fourteen projects against the same criteria opened up many observations and insights. Approximately twenty of the seventy-two attributes in Stephen Kellert's list were not addressed in the case studies; in addition, some of the attributes were more frequently addressed than others.

LIGHT + SPACE

- **Natural light** ●●●●
- **Filtered and diffused light** ●●
- **Light and shadow** ●●●●●
- Reflected light
- Light pools
- Warm light
- **Light as shape and form** ●●
- **Spaciousness** ●●●●
- **Spatial variability** ●●●●
- Space as shape and form
- Spatial harmony
- **Inside-outside spaces** ●●●●●●

PLACE-BASED RELATIONSHIPS

- **Geographic connection to place** ●
- **Historic connection to place** ●
- **Ecological connection to place** ●●●●
- **Cultural connection to place** ●●
- **Indigenous materials** ●●●
- **Landscape orientation** ●●
- **Landscape features that define building form** ●●●
- **Landscape ecology** ●●●●
- **Integration of culture and ecology** ●●●●
- **Spirit of place** ●●●●
- **Avoiding placelessness** ●

EVOLVED HUMAN-NATURE RELATIONSHIPS

- **Prospect and refuge** ●●
- **Order and complexity** ●
- **Curiosity and enticement** ●●●●
- **Change and metamorphosis** ●
- **Security and protection** ●
- Mastery and control
- Affection and attachment
- **Attraction and beauty** ●
- **Exploration and discovery** ●●
- Information and cognition
- Fear and awe
- **Reverence and spirituality** ●

Some of the attributes that were most frequently featured, such as Light and Shadow, Central Focal Point, and Ecological Connection to Place, were key in connecting the building to its place and its community. Such themes are fundamental for all projects to effectively integrate biophilic design and are vital to their success.

Many of the attributes within the Natural Shapes and Forms element were underrepresented or not represented at all. This reflects the standardization of building materials. Throughout the building supply industry, wood and steel are cut and molded almost exclusively into linear dimensions and rectangular forms. As a result, buildings designed today are predominantly composed of straight lines and right angles in response to market-available components and materials. In striking contrast, the natural elegance of VanDusen Botanical Garden Visitor Centre, with its curving walls and petal-like roof, demonstrates the powerful draw of natural forms.

LESSER-KNOWN ATTRIBUTES

NATURAL PATTERNS + PROCESSES

Sensory variability

Information richness

Age, change and the patina of time

Growth and efflorescence

Central focal point

Patterned wholes

Bounded spaces

Transitional spaces

Linked series and chains

Integration of parts to wholes

Complementary contrasts

Dynamic balance and tension

Fractals

Hierarchically organized ratios and scales

EVOLVED HUMAN-NATURE RELATIONSHIPS

Prospect and refuge

Order and complexity

Curiosity and enticement

Change and metamorphosis

Security and protection

Mastery and control

Affection and attachment

Attraction and beauty

Exploration and discovery

Information and cognition

Fear and awe

Reverence and spirituality

Several attributes within the Natural Patterns and Processes element were not referenced in these projects. Attributes such as Growth and Efflorescence and Patterned Wholes require a deliberate design intention that is most likely not required by the function or program of most buildings. Within the element of Evolved Human-Nature Relationships, Affection and Attachment and Fear and Awe were not demonstrated by any of the case studies but clearly represent important and powerful relationships that people experience in their homes and places of worship.

It became clear that Natural Patterns and Processes and Evolved Human-Nature Relationships are the lesser-known and used biophilic design elements. The attributes within these elements mostly reference the psychological connection between people and nature and the ways in which we instinctively react and respond to spaces, whether they be man-made or natural. For many people, these attributes may seem like abstract concepts; however, the lesser-known biophilic design elements represent a significant opportunity for designers to enrich spaces for people by deeply reinforcing the fact that they are part of nature. Including curiosity and beauty in buildings, for example, makes people happier and helps ensure that these buildings will endure and survive the test of time.

Bertschi School Science Wing

KEY LESSONS LEARNED

Each of the fourteen projects took a different design approach. Some teams utilized biophilic design to drive their design thinking and concept development; some came to it during design; and still others had already embedded this approach into the way their practice designs every project. Through analyzing all of these projects, some key lessons have emerged:

START EARLY: The project teams that integrated biophilic design early on—the ones that fully embraced it as a genuine design driver and educated themselves on the depth of knowledge and available research—were the most successful in creating places where people and nature can thrive together.

COLLABORATION: Teams that took a collaborative approach were the most successful at implementing biophilic design. Since everyone relates to nature to some degree, biophilic design represents "common ground" where disparate team members can connect. By making an earnest effort to dive deeply into biophilic design together, teams can create shared goals in which every member is invested.

CHALLENGE THE NORMAL PROCESS: Typically, building design is based on a response to its functions, physical site limitations, and preconceived design aesthetic. Biophilic design has the potential to turn the usual way of designing a building upside down. The teams that let biophilic design drive their design concepts and decisions were the most successful.

DON'T RESIST: With so many economic demands and conventional practice pressures on design teams and owners already, it might be tempting to pay lip service to biophilic design. However, if practitioners treat biophilic design as yet another set of requirements to simply "get through," they will miss out on the opportunity to explore the rich palette of inspiration that biophilic design offers.

BEST PRACTICE PROCESS

Given the assessment of these fourteen projects, I recommend the following process for teams seeking to integrate biophilic design into their projects.

AT PROJECT START:

1. Before putting pen to paper, hold a deep immersion day during which all team members explore biophilic design together. Walk or camp on the site as a team. Seek to understand the true nature of the place from a cultural, climate, ecological and historical perspective. Ask questions: What is the ecology of this place? What is its history? How does climate shape the land, and how do other living creatures respond to it?

2. Bring the whole team up to the same level of knowledge about biophilic design through immersing them in educational resources and case studies. To shake up the usual way of designing a building, explore as a team the potential for incorporating the "lesser known" elements of biophilic design.

3. Include unconventional disciplines and groups—public artists, biologists, ecologists and indigenous communities, to name a few—who can help the team see the psychology of place from a different perspective.

4. Capture the ideas in a framework that can serve as a roadmap for the project throughout all phases.

CONCEPTUAL DESIGN:

1. Develop profiles of the users of the building; think about how each of them will arrive and leave the project. How many times and in what ways will they interact with nature, from the time they arrive to the time they leave the building?

2. Will every occupant know the time of day, weather and season at every moment and in all spaces throughout the building, and how?

3. What is the regional material palette and how can it be used to construct the building? How will these materials express the ecology of place?

4. How are the "lesser known" attributes being experienced in the building? Test the floor plan against each one.

DESIGN DOCUMENTS:

1. Keep testing the design against the "lesser known" biophilic design elements. Can the floor plan be enriched by creating transitional spaces of linked series and chains, for example?

2. Is the building responding to place and climate? If it is, the energy demand should be almost non-existent in the energy model.

3. Does every person have access to fresh air and daylight?

4. How are indigenous and regional materials being used to express connection to place?

ASSESSMENT:

1. Make a plan for continual assessment of the framework through all design phases that is integrated into project meetings and processes and holds all team members accountable.

THROUGHOUT:

Go outside as much as possible, without each person forming a relationship with nature, biophilic design will not be possible.

Google Chicago

CONCLUSION

Thinking about buildings as a journey of experiences opens up exciting and new possibilities for the design and architecture fields. Biophilic design holds the potential for bringing renewed inspiration and curiosity both to how we create our spaces and to how we engage with them as habitats.

As humans become increasingly disconnected from nature in our daily lives, the task of connecting people and nature in our built environment becomes even more urgent. Doing so will require intentional action, and we will have to purposefully unlearn some of our habitual ways of designing and constructing buildings. However, as these modern and historic case studies show, we already possess the tools. We do not need to develop new technologies or invest in research and development to make biophilic buildings possible—the only barrier is our reluctance to change.

We already value buildings and spaces that connect us to nature, as we demonstrate by our willingness to pay a premium for such buildings. Enlightened designers and owners understand that biophilic buildings are a good investment. There is a sound economic argument for biophilic design, particularly when health and productivity of employees is taken into account. Buildings created in harmony with nature are valued by people because they allow us to be healthier and happier. With so few technological barriers and with ever more research quantifying the benefits of biophilic design— and now, with an emerging set of resources that demonstrate and elaborate on how to create biophilic buildings—I predict a groundswell of support for the practice of biophilic design. We must be the conduit by which biophilic design reaches the broader building community by introducing its concepts and illustrating its benefits, and especially by embracing its practice. If each one of us makes the commitment to let biophilic design guide the design and construction of our buildings, we can truly create the change we seek.

RESOURCES

MULTISENSORY EXPERIENCES

These fourteen case studies are just the start. At www.living-future.org/biophilic-design/ a wide range of resources are being developed to provide sample frameworks, charrette agendas and multi-sensory and multi-media tools that will allow you to be immersed in these projects and many more in the future and incorporate their lessons learned into your future projects.

EDUCATION

BIOPHILIC WEBINARS:
living-future.org/education/5-part-series-biophilic-design/

ILFI LEARNING PAGE:
living-future.org/online-learning/

The five-part Series includes the following courses (which are also offered individually):
1. Introduction to Biophilic Design
2. Terrapin Bright Green Tools and Resources
3. Biophilic Case Studies
4. Biophilia Research
5. Multi-Sensory Products

MOVIES

- *Biophilic Design: The Architecture of Life* Directed by Stephen R. Kellert and Bill Finnegan. Tamarack Media, 2011. DVD.

BOOKS

- Wilson, Edward O. *Biophilia*. Harvard University Press, 1984.

- Kellert, Stephen R, and Edward O Wilson. *The Biophilia Hypothesis*, Island Press, 1995.

- Kellert, Stephen R. *Building for Life: Designing and Understanding the Human-Nature Connection*, Island Press, 2005.

- Kellert, Stephen R; Judith, Heerwagen, and Martin Mador. *Biophilic Design: The Theory, Science, and Practice of Bringing Buildings to Life,* John Wiley, 2008.

- Kellert, Stephen R. *Birthright: People and Nature in the Modern World*, Yale University Press, 2012.

- Kellert, Stephen R, and Elizabeth F. Calabrese. *The Practice of Biophilic Design,* www.biophilic-design.com 2015.

TERRAPIN REPORTS

- Terrapin Bright Green. 2014. *The Economics of Biophilia: Why designing with nature in mind makes financial sense.* Terrapin Bright Green. www.terrapinbrightgreen.com/report/economics-of-biophilia/.

- Terrapin Bright Green. 2014. *14 Patterns of Biophilic Design: Improving Health and Well-Being in the Built Environment.* www.terrapinbrightgreen.com/report/14-patterns/.

- Terrapin Bright Green. 2015. *Biophilic Case Studies.* Terrapin Bright Green. www.terrapinbrightgreen.com/report/biophilic-design-case-studies/.

- Salingaros, Nikos & Ryan, Catherine. 2015. *Biophilia & Healing Environments: Healthy Principles for Designing the Built World.* Terrapin Bright Green & Metropolis Magazine. www.terrapinbrightgreen.com/report/biophilia-healing-environments/.

RESEARCH

- Annerstedt, Matilda, Peter Jönsson, Mattias Wallergård, Gerd Johansson, Björn Karlson, Patrik Grahn, Åse Marie Hansen, and Peter Währborg. "Inducing physiological stress recovery with sounds of nature in a virtual reality forest — Results from a pilot study." Physiology & Behavior 118 (May 2013): 240-50. doi:10.1016/j.physbeh.2013.05.023.

- Baicker, K., D. Cutler, and Z. Song. "Workplace Wellness Programs Can Generate Savings." *Health Affairs*

29, no. 2 (February 2010): 304-11. doi:10.1377/hlthaff.2009.0626.

- Choi, Joon-Ho, and Vivian Loftness. "Investigation of human body skin temperatures as a bio-signal to indicate overall thermal sensations." *Building and Environment 58* (July 2012): 258-69. doi:10.1016/j.buildenv.2012.07.003.

- Horr, Yousef Al, Mohammed Arif, Martha Katafygiotou, Ahmed Mazroei, Amit Kaushik, and Esam Elsarrag. "Impact of indoor environmental quality on occupant well-being and comfort: A review of the literature." *International Journal of Sustainable Built Environment 5, no. 1* (June 2016): 1-11. doi:10.1016/j.ijsbe.2016.03.006.

- Lee, Kate E., Kathryn J.h. Williams, Leisa D. Sargent, Nicholas S.g. Williams, and Katherine A. Johnson. "40-second green roof views sustain attention: The role of micro-breaks in attention restoration." *Journal of Environmental Psychology 42* (May 2015): 182-89. doi:10.1016/j.jenvp.2015.04.003.

- Macnaughton, Piers, James Pegues, Usha Satish, Suresh Santanam, John Spengler, and Joseph Allen. "Economic, Environmental and Health Implications of Enhanced Ventilation in Office Buildings." *International Journal of Environmental Research and Public Health 12, no. 12* (November 2015): 14709-4722. doi:10.3390/ijerph121114709.

- Tanner, C. Kenneth. "The influence of school architecture on academic achievement." *Journal of Educational Administration 38*, no. 4 (February 2000): 309-30. doi:10.1108/09578230010373598.

"This is the bright home
in which I live,
this is where
I ask
my friends
to come,
this is where I want
to love all the things
it has taken me so long
to learn to love.

This is the temple
of my adult aloneness
and I belong
to that aloneness
as I belong to my life.

There is no house
like the house of belonging."

DAVID WHYTE

INTERNATIONAL LIVING FUTURE INSTITUTE:

The International Living Future Institute (ILFI) is a hub for visionary programs. ILFI offers global strategies for lasting sustainability, partnering with local communities to create grounded and relevant solutions, including green building and infrastructure solutions on scales ranging from single room renovations to neighborhoods or whole cities. ILFI administers the Living Building Challenge, the built environment's most rigorous and ambitious performance standard. It is the parent organization for Cascadia Green Building Council, a chapter of both the United States and Canada Green Building Councils that serves Alaska, British Columbia, Washington and Oregon. It is also home to Ecotone Publishing, a unique publishing house dedicated to telling the story of the green building movement's pioneering thinkers and practitioners.

BIOPHILIC DESIGN INITIATIVE:

The International Living Future Institute has seen a demonstrated need among the Living Building Challenge community for Biophilic Design resources that can take the practice from theory to reality. While progress has been made to communicate what Biophilic Design is and to demonstrate why it is crucial to a Living Future, very little has been made around the process of how to achieve it. The International Living Future Institute has brought together leading experts in the field to form an Advisory Task Force that leads the initiative through collaboration and inclusion of existing resources. The Biophilic Design Initiative aims to achieve the goal of broad adoption of Biophilic Design among the design community, building owners, communities, and cities.

LIVING BUILDING CHALLENGE:

The Living Building Challenge is the built environment's most rigorous performance standard. It calls for the creation of building projects at all scales that operate as cleanly, beautifully, and efficiently as nature's architecture. To be certified under the Challenge, projects must meet a series of ambitious performance requirements, including net zero energy, waste, and water, over a minimum of twelve months of continuous occupancy.

ECOTONE PUBLISHING:

Founded by green building experts in 2004, Ecotone Publishing is dedicated to meeting the growing demand for authoritative and accessible books on sustainable design, materials selection and building techniques in North America and beyond. Ecotone searches out and documents inspiring projects, visionary people, and innovative trends that are leading the design industry to transformational change toward a healthier planet.

PHOTOGRAPHY:

Reggie Alvey: p.23

Jeremy Bitterman courtesy of EHDD: p.124, 126, 128, 131

Jeremy Bitterman courtesy of Joni L. Jonecki & Associates: p.120, 123

Courtesy of Bohlin Cywinski Jackson: p.52, 55-60, 62-63

Courtesy of Bruner/Cott & Associates: p.74, 76, 79-81, 83-84

Felipe Castilho: p.21

Brian Chisholm courtesy of Google: p.176, 178-186

Jack Clark courtesy of the Mosaic Centre for Conscious Community and Commerce: p.96, 103, 104

Brian Cohen: p.42

Curtis Comeau Photography: p.100-101

Courtesy of Connect Landscape: p.6, 118

Denmarsh Photography, Inc: p.45, 47, 50

Ana Dermer: p.134, 135, 142

Brian Donovan: p.19

Dan Farmer courtesy of the Bullitt Center: p.12, 166, 172, 174

Courtesy of Flansburgh Architects: p.86-91, 93-94

Franco Folini, Wikimedia Commons: P.114

Courtesy of Glumac Shanghai Office: p.8, 144, 146-153

John Gollings Photography: p.3, 154, 156-158, 160-165

Jake Ingle, Unsplash: p.188-189

Courtesy of Jasmax: p.138, 141

Courtesy of Joni L. Jonecki & Associates: p.122

Kris Knutson courtesy of Joni L. Jonecki & Associates: p.127, 199

Courtesy of Lake | Flato Architects: p.26, 64-73

Nic Lehoux courtesy of the Bullitt Center: p.168-173, 176, 191

Nic Lehoux courtesy of Perkins + Will: pg.108-113, 115, 116, 119

Terry Lorant courtesy of the David & Lucile Packard Foundation: p.129

Tom Marks courtesy of The Bertschi School: p.32-41, 195, 197

Jirka Matousek: p.22, 24

Courtesy of the Mosaic Centre for Conscious Community and Commerce: p.98, 99, 102, 107

David Olsen: p.15, 132, 139, 140, 143

Courtesy of Phipps Center for Sustainable Landscapes: p.48

Perry Quan: p.25

Steve Richey, Unsplash: p.30-31

Zachary Staines, Unsplash: p.202-203

Amanda Sturgeon: p.136

Kristine Weilert, Unsplash: p.16-17

Paul g. Wiegman: p.11, 44, 51

Scott Worthington: p.20